Never Cooked Before

Gotta Cook Now!™

A Total Guide for the Beginning Cook

by Leonard F. Charla

Countinghouse Press, Inc.

Bloomfield Hills, Michigan

Never Cooked Before

Gotta Cook Now!™

A Total Guide for the Beginning Cook

by Leonard F. Charla

Countinghouse Press, Inc.

Bloomfield Hills, Michigan 48301

© 1999, by Leonard F. Charla
Illustrations © 1999 by Leonard F. Charla

All rights reserved. No part of this book may be reproduced or utilized in any form or by any means, electronic or mechanical, including photocopying, imaging, recording or by any information storage or retrieval system without permission in writing from the publisher. The trademarks used in this book are the properties of the respective trademark owners.

Address inquiries to

Countinghouse Press, Inc.
311, 6632 Telegraph Road
Bloomfield Hills, Michigan 48301.

Phones: Voice: 248.642.7191;   FAX: 248.642.7192.

First edition.

First Printing

Library of Congress Catalog Card Number: 98-093626

ISBN: 0-9664732-0-5

Printed in the United States of America by Thompson-Shore, Inc., Dexter, MI
Cover design by Sans Serif, Inc., Saline, MI

Dedication: For Elizabeth, Larisa, and Christopher

Acknowledgements

Many folks helped with this book. Elizabeth A. DuMouchelle provided running commentary and daily encouragement, in addition to unerring guidance on cooking and baking principles. Larisa Charla Breton edited with a sharp pencil, and Christopher Charla provided many hours of computer and layout assistance. Friends and relatives were generous with recipes, tips, suggestions, encouragement and comments.

Special thanks to Edward Cantlin, Barbara Cash, Josephine Charla, Mary L. Charla, Izora Cohl, Sanford Cohl, Laura Fitzpatrick, Charles Flynn, Pauline Flynn, Tim Flynn, Wendy Good, Sharon Hatchett, Lee Hoffman, Joanne Isbey, Beth Jordan, Larry Jordan, Bronwyn Lindsay, Margaret Lorusso, Csilla Luckett, Ed Luckett, Carolyn Marino, Ann Murray, Joy Nachman, Mary O'Herron, Gay Ohlrich, Delbert Lee Petersen, Carl Proffer, Ellendea Proffer, Alice Schultes, Carrie Shepherd, Brad Stocker, Marilyn Stocker, and Estelle Tyner. This book would not have been possible without them. Any errors or omissions are the responsibility of the author.

DISCLAIMER

This is a book of information. It does not claim to be, and is not, medical or nutritional advice. For medical advice, consult a physician; for nutritional advice, consult a nutritionist. If this is not acceptable to you, the publisher will refund the full price of the book upon written request.

Contents

Introduction		7
Chapter 1	Welcome to the Kitchen	19
Chapter 2	Stocking Up for Week One	35
Chapter 3	Menus and Recipes for Week One	55
Chapter 4	Stocking Up for Week Two	97
Chapter 5	Menus and Recipes for Week Two	101
Chapter 6	Stocking Up for Week Three	131
Chapter 7	Menus and Recipes for Week Three	137
Chapter 8	Stocking Up for Week Four	161
Chapter 9	Menus and Recipes for Week Four	167
Chapter 10	Stocking Up for Week Five	197
Chapter 11	Menus and Recipes for Week Five	205
Chapter 12	Additional Menus and Recipes; Cleaning Up	231
Recipe Index		239
Index		242

Books in The Gotta Cook Now!™ Series

Never Cooked Before/Gotta Cook Now!™

Gotta Cook Now!™ Goes Italian

Gotta Cook Now!™ Goes Mexican

Introduction

"The Hungries" Hit You Yet Again

It's mealtime, and you're hungry again. And this time, you are *really* tired of fast food, of carry-out, of bar food, or; that stuff is fine, but you are *really* tired of all that expense. Or it's raining and your favorite place doesn't deliver, and you are really tired of *that*. Or you are on your own, and the words "what's next?" suddenly appear on life's display screen and the answer is,

"I'm hungry."

In short, "I've never cooked before. But I've gotta cook now." It is finally time to tackle cooking. Cooking as a skill. Cooking as a social tool. Cooking (maybe) as a hobby. Cooking (just possibly) as an art. Not just microwave popcorn, or frozen dinners, or even warmed up "doggie bags" from last night's restaurant, but real food, that tastes good, looks great, is easy to prepare, and makes sense. But where to start?

If that's where you are, this book is for you.

Who Are You?

Maybe you're in high school, and you've decided to learn how to cook since it's something a large number of adults you know seem to do.

College Student?

Perhaps you're a college or university student or new graduate in your first apartment, and you're interested in saving time, saving money, and eating well.

Divorced?

You might be divorced or widowed, and suddenly confronted with the need to go it alone in the kitchen.

New hobby?

You may be someone who's always had a desire to cook, and now you've reached a point in your career where it looks like some cooking might be fun.

Suddenly on your own?

You may be on your own, for any of a number of reasons, after a lot of years in a relationship where someone else did the cooking.

Whoever you are, and wherever you are in your life,

Welcome to This Book!

No matter why you're reading this, welcome! Cooking for yourself is interesting. It is fun to assemble ingredients, put them through the cooking process, and wind up with a great meal. It is, over time, much more economical than eating in restaurants. And by cooking for yourself you'll be able to provide great nutritional benefits, and save time as well.

You can do it!

If you can follow a pro football game, you can cook. Reading the recipe is receiving the ball, preparing it is a couple of first downs and a completed pass, and putting the meal on the table is the touchdown. It is a question of focusing on the goal, which in this case is cooking good meals, and following a few procedures.

What this book is about

Quite simply, this book is about cooking if you've never really cooked before. Whether you're alone, part of a couple, or a larger household, this book shows you how to prepare really good meals, in a really practical and easy way.

What This Book Does

Lays out the basic equipment needed to get started;

Lists what to buy, what to keep in on hand in your pantry, and what should be purchased more frequently;

Provides more than one month's (five weeks, actually) worth of menus, with recipes;

Has a recipe for each new item in each menu, with serving techniques, where you need them;

Talks about timing and having each item at hand when you are ready for it;

Shows how to serve a meal, and provides handy tips for preparation, presentation, serving, cleanup and storage.

Shows you how planning ahead can save time and make life easier and better.

Explains the cooking "mysteries," lists common mistakes, and how to avoid them.

Contains great ideas and recipes for leftovers.

By giving you the ability to run a kitchen and cook your own meals, helps you get control over your life and make informed choices about *when* you want to eat, *where* you want to eat, *what* you want to eat, and *how* you want to eat it.

What This Book Doesn't Do

No single cookbook does everything. (That's why there are thousands of them.) Using this book:

doesn't make you a gourmet;

doesn't provide more than the basic skills for cooking; and

doesn't turn you into "Chef Wizard."

But, hey--the food you will learn to prepare using this book will taste really good, cost much less than restaurant food of the same quality, a will be attractive, appetizing, tasty and fresh; and will very likely improve the quality of your life.

Used on a consistent basis, this book will help you eat really well, on your own terms, at significant savings over the cost of restaurant meals. As we said, no one is going to confuse you with one of The Great Cooks of The World. You can become one of them, though, if you want to, and this book can start you on your way.

"Political" Issues

Vegetarian or not, animal rights or not, high fat v. low fat, salt or not, alcohol or not--all these are issues, real issues, of real concern. But they are not among the primary concerns of this cookbook.

Ideas for meals lower in fat and salt

Still, lots of folks are interested in lowering fat, sugar and salt intakes, and for that reason, many of the recipes in this book will contain low-fat or low-salt alternatives. In many recipes, salt is listed as "optional." Some shopping lists and recipes will be followed by "low-fat alternative" or "healthy eating ideas" suggestions for lower fat or lower salt variations. And recipes that are low in fat, or low in salt, or both, will say so. Where recipes call for wine or spirits, those ingredients are frequently optional and can be omitted or other flavors substituted.

Some basic assumptions

This cookbook assumes you are:

relatively normal;

relatively healthy; and that you will maintain a

relatively balanced lifestyle.

So, some of the recipes are vegetarian; others use one or more of red meat, poultry, fish, or dairy products as ingredients. Many recipes call for butter, oils, or other fats, and many list sugar or salt or both as ingredients. Why? Because all of the foregoing when *used in moderation* are, in the opinion of the author, just fine.

The core secrets

Remember "Old Aunt Rose?" Old Aunt Rose learned to cook at her mother's knee, never read a recipe in her life, cooked with "a little of this and a little of that,"and was always ready to feed whoever showed up at her table, whether one or twenty. Somehow, there was always enough and it was always great. We now reveal the *core secrets* of Old Aunt Rose's wizardry:

1) she was *organized;* and 2) she was *interactive.*

Yes, organized. First, she knew how long different foods took to cook; secondly, she knew what ingredients went into what dishes; then, she knew which dishes went with which other dishes; and finally, she knew about how many people each dish would serve.

That's right, interactive. Over the years, Aunt Rose had internalized and integrated all this information, experience, and data. She learned you can "stretch" soup with a couple of extra carrots, and, say, some rice and a bit more water. She learned what went with what, and how long it all took. She, as they would say now, "got it all together." You can, too.

Use Whatever Works

On the other hand, Aunt Rose and her peers *spent lots and lots of time cooking*. Chances are, you don't have that kind of time. Well, things have changed. Food styles have changed. Products have changed. Cooking methods have changed. And the times, they have a-changed. (Aunt Rose seldom 'nuked' items in her microwave and she never used dried onion soup mix, either). Guess what:

This book uses anything that works.

Microwaves are okay.
Frozen foods are okay.
Dried soup mixes are okay.
Mixed salad greens from the produce section are okay.
And so forth.

Microwave and convection ovens are excellent tools. Dried onion soup mix, when you follow package directions, makes a really good soup. Or a good party dip, if you've got some sour cream or yogurt. Or a great sauce base. Convenience foods have never been better. Food processors are terrific. Frozen foods taste surprisingly good, and in some cases are better than fresh. Baking mixes save lots of time and yield great results.

Actually, you would be surprised at what Aunt Rose would be doing, if she were still around. And, by the way, while you're learning, *unlike* Aunt Rose,

Be sure to measure all ingredients.

(Call that this book's first useful tip. Future tips will say **"Tip:"** in front of them.)

The Six Steps to a Winning Meal

To put it another way, think of every meal as the result of five or six steps you've taken, or at least considered:

1. Plan it--plan the meal or snack you intend to eat;

2. Get it--obtain the food, by purchasing it or growing it, or possibly even gathering, hunting or fishing it;

3. Store it--in the refrigerator, the freezer, the pantry, or a bread box or fruit bowl;

4. Prep it--including some, but probably not all of the following: wash it, cool it, peel it, clean it, filet it, freeze it, chop it, mince it, dice it, slice it, roll it and pat it and mark it with "T." Of course, in some instances, such as a bag of potato chips, your prep is simply opening the package;

5. Cook it--which includes the following possibilities and plenty of others: bake it, blanch it, boil it, braise it, fry it, poach it, saute it, heat it, thaw it, microwave it. And yes, you can skip this step in the case of foods that are sometimes eaten uncooked, such as many fruits and vegetables;

6. Serve it--on a platter or a plate, a bowl or a tureen, in a casserole or serving dish.

Serving methods

Today it is common in many homes for serving dishes to be brought to the table for each diner to serve herself or himself; in many restaurants, each diner is served his or her own plate that already contains the meal (or course). But each method of serving can be used in either arena.

When restaurants bring serving platters to a table for diners to serve themselves, they often refer to this manner of service as "family style." (However, when my grandmother brought individual plates heaped with food to the table, she did not refer to her mode of service as "restaurant style.")

Here are some suggestions on how to approach a week's worth of meals.

1. Plan it

At the beginning of your week, stop for a few minutes and decide what you'd like to eat that week. This doesn't have to be an elaborate, detailed plan. Just choose a few main dishes or entrees and go on from there. Write these down--this is the beginning of your shopping list. Some meals, such as meat loaf, can make great leftovers, and this is something you can include in your planning. For example, serve the meat loaf plain, with potatoes the first time, and with a tomato sauce or brown gravy and rice the second time. This avoids the "boredom factor."

If you are cooking for just one or two people, buy most foods in the smallest sizes available. This is more costly on a per-ounce or per-pound basis, but saves lots of money in the long run, since far less food is wasted.

2. Get it

How often will you be getting to the store? If it's once a week, plan your menu so that the most perishable items will be consumed first. Fish and poultry, for example, don't store well, so they should be prepared and consumed shortly after you purchase them. If you are going to be shopping more than once a week, it makes buying perishable items a bit easier. Some vegetables, such as onions, potatoes, carrots, and cabbage have a longer storage life than others.

3. Store it

A good refrigerator is a must for keeping cold things cold and frozen things frozen. Generally, the bottom shelf in the back is the coldest part of the refrigerator. Potatoes, onions, yams, and garlic are vegetables that lend themselves to pantry storage rather than refrigerator storage. Bread boxes are okay for storing bread, but if you're cooking for just one person, and not consuming a lot of bread, it stores wonderfully in the refrigerator, and can also be frozen.

4. Prep it

This is easier than it sounds. When you peel a banana, you're "prepping" or preparing it to be eaten. Some foods need more prep than others. Sliced bread can simply be taken from the wrapper, and a stick of butter can be unwrapped, placed in a butter dish and left to come to room temperature. On the other hand, vegetables need to be washed, and some of them need to be peeled.

Short of time? Use frozen vegetables, or fresh ones that have been prepped for you at the super market, such as baby carrots that have been washed and peeled. Generally, rinse poultry and fish in cold water and pat it dry with paper towels. It makes for easier sauteing. Most of the recipes in this book will talk about prepping or will call for foods that have been prepped.

5. *Cook it*

There are many ways to cook, and it's a good idea to try them all, to see which methods suit you and produce the best results. Lots of folks swear by grilling, and it produces hearty flavor. Baking a casserole in the oven provides time for the cook to accomplish other tasks, such as setting the table and making the salad. Sauteing or frying provides great flavor, but like grilling, requires the cook's constant attention.

Like practicing interceptions, the more you do it, the better you'll get. You'll discover that the more things, ways, and methods you try, and the more times you attempt them, the better you'll become. And, yes, you'll have failures. They're part of the learning process. One guy, cooking for the first time for his two-year-old and five-year-old, put two cups of vinegar into a cake mix instead of two teaspoonsful of vinegar. The kids never let him forget it, and the only creature that ate the results was the dog, but on the other hand, he never made that mistake again. And twenty years later, the kids now come back to his house and say, "Dad, will you cook us one of your dinners?"

6. *Serve it*

The concept of serving also includes the concept of *presentation,* or "how does it look?" In a movie once the hostess at a dinner said something like "Pass all those cartons of Chinese take-out food down here, they look better when they're lined up." That's one approach to presentation. Others may be more formal. But generally, you want food you've prepared and cooked to look pleasant and appetizing.

Table settings are not all that complicated

Over the years, this "presentation" goal, which is shared by millions, has evolved into certain conventions, such as a table that has been set, with napkins, flatware, plates and glasses in generally defined places.

Four-line explanation

Do not let these serving conventions intimidate you. They are not rocket science. Almost all table settings can be explained in just four lines:

1. Knives and spoons on right, forks on left.
2. Napkin on left, glass or cup on right, above knife.
3. Place the utensils you'll be using first on the outside.
4. During the meal, work your way in from the outside utensil.

No big deal.

"Spin control"

You can do other things to point the meal in a certain direction, and influence its "spin."

"Add to the appeal"

The table-setting conventions can be enhanced by other objects that add to the appeal of the food, such as candles, flowers, tablecloths and flattering lighting. These things can be used to set the mood for the meal.

And while this is a book about cooking, and not a dating book, putting a couple of candles on the table, along with some flowers you picked up at the supermarket really impresses a date. The gender of the date doesn't matter, nor do the date's verbal skills. Even the most phlegmatic types notice. You married guys might really be surprised when you try this and discover your wife looks at you through new eyes.

At any rate, you might want subdued lighting and soft background music for a quiet dinner; plastic plates and cups for having the gang over to watch a game; and bold accessories for a zippy breakfast.

Easy Meals First

This book is set up with the easiest and least complex recipes at the beginning of the book, followed by more difficult, elaborate, or more complicated recipes. That way, you'll gain confidence as you go along, and the skills you learn in the early part of the book will come in handy as you move through the rest of the book.

Substitutes and Second Stringers

Lots of times, the suggested foods can be replaced. For instance, if the menu suggests using frozen broccoli as the vegetable, but all that's in the house is a can of green beans, they'll do just fine. If your star is benched, bring on the second stringer.

Chapter One

Getting Started

The Basic Basics: Tools of the Trade; Kitchen Terms; Measurements; Substitutions

HERE you are in the kitchen. Before anyone, even Aunt Rose, can begin cooking, certain basic fixtures, appliances, furniture, equipment and tools need to be in place. For cooking now, you'll need the following fixtures, appliances, furniture, equipment, and tools:

Fixtures and furniture

You'll need: a sink with running water; some flat work space (table top or counter top, or both) is a good idea; a table and a couple of chairs are not *absolutely* necessary, but are very helpful.

Basic appliances

Some basic appliances are absolutely essential including a stove, and a refrigerator with freezer compartment and at least two ice cube trays.

Optional appliances

Some appliances are useful but not absolutely necessary. If you have an automatic under-counter or mobile dishwasher, that's great. However, Western civilization did manage to do without them for about 10,000 years, and they've been around for only about 45 or 50, so it's just possible one can survive *sans* dishwasher. (The final chapter in this book talks about cleaning up. With automatic dishwashers. And without them.)

Campers may get along with less furniture, appliances, fixtures and equipment. But we're talking about cooking meals on a going-forward basis, in the same place, over a long period of time. One other thing--that stove, that sink, that refrigerator--they need to be in working order.

Really useful, but not strictly necessary, are:

a microwave oven;

a toaster or toaster oven;

a low-priced barbecue grill (for use outdoors).

Some of the recipes in this book can be prepared using either a conventional stove or a microwave (or a toaster oven) and where this is possible, the recipes will let you know.

Utensils, cookware and tableware, or "Tools of the Trade"

Pots, pans, baking items, serving dishes, and storage pieces should include the items listed below. It's a long list, but take courage. An important fact to remember is:

You do not need all these things at once.

If your life style resembles that of the attic dwellers in Puccini's *La Boheme*, and you're burning your manuscripts for fuel, you can start with:

a cast iron frying pan; and a large spoon.

(You can even make coffee in the frying pan, if you need to do so.) Probably, you are not quite that impoverished. So, the next two things you would want, assuming absolute or near-destitution, would be:

a saucepan;

a knife;

a fork.

you're off! Anyway, *after* the frying pan, spoon, saucepan, knife and fork, begin to acquire:

3 frying pans, preferably cast iron, in 10 inch, 8 inch, and 6 inch diameters;

1 nonstick frying pan, 8 inch diameter;

3 saucepans, 1.5, 2.5, and 4 cup capacities. The 2.5 cup saucepan should have a cover. Stainless steel is a good bet;

3 measuring cups. Useful capacity measuring cups are 1 cup, 2 cup, and 4 or 4 and 1/2 cup sizes;

a bunch of measuring spoons, from 1/8 teaspoon (tsp.), in graduated sizes, through 1 tablespoon (Tbs.);

1 cookie sheet. Great for cookies, as well as biscuits and rolls; even better: two or more cookie sheets;

3 glass or ceramic baking dishes, with covers, in graduated sizes. These can go from the freezer or refrigerator into the oven or microwave. Make sure one of them is about 8" x 8" x 2" (the most useful size). The biggest one should hold about 4 to 4 and 1/2 quarts. They are great for casseroles, good for storing leftovers, and if they are attractive, you can serve from them;

one 9" x 9" x 2" open baking pan, metal or heat-resistant glass;

one 9" x 13" x 2" open baking pan (a larger capacity pan);

three or four mixing bowls, in graduated sizes;

two large sized spoons, for mixing and serving;

one flexible spatula or bowl scraper (if it's plastic, don't use it on hot pots or pans);

four or five good work knives. You need a paring knife, for small vegetable and fruit work; a slicing knife; a carving knife; a bread knife; and a knife that can be used for chopping;

mixing tools. At a minimum, a mechanical egg beater is useful; if you can afford it, also get a small electric mixer and one or two wire whisks. Whisks are good for small jobs such as whipping cream. Electric mixers are hard to beat when it comes to larger jobs such as cake batter. If you can afford a food processor, get one of them, as well. They are good for mixing and cutting.

one pancake turner (good for burgers and steaks, too);

one 2 to 2.5 quart pitcher (for juice, iced tea, wine, or beer);

one can opener

a colander (bowl-shaped strainer); if you get a fine screen or fine wire mesh one, you can use it to sift dry ingredients, too;

two good quality pot holders (also called "hot pads);

a corkscrew, for opening bottles of wine and other corked items;

a potato peeler;

two round 9-inch cake pans;

a four-sided grater

a sponge or two, for cleanup;

one or two plastic scouring pads, for cleaning items that have acquired a crust during the cooking process;

two or three dish rags, about 9 inches by 9 inches;

two or three dish towels, about 18 inches x 24 inches;

a dish rack and portable drainboard (optional if you have an automatic dishwasher);

powdered dishwasher detergent (for automatic dishwashers);

a bar or two of hand soap, for washing hands after handling items like poultry or fish;

a bottle of liquid dishwasher detergent for small cleanup jobs if you have an automatic dishwasher and big jobs if you don't. (See Chapter 12 for information, strategies, and tips on cleaning up.)

Well, what about egg slicers, double boilers, pressure cookers, pastry tubes, a flour sifter, a demi tasse set, and a cake holder? And what about other items, gadgets, specialty utensils and dishes that one might use in the kitchen? Well, those things are all good to have. They are less urgently needed at first. It's fun to pick them up now and again, as they become useful or desired.

Where to get all this? Department stores, hardware stores, and kitchen supply stores all carry these items. If you're on a budget, try yard sales or your folks' attic. Don't buy a second-hand microwave or toaster unless you have a qualified repair person check those items out thoroughly.

Heads up: unplug small electrical appliances before repairing or cleaning them. (See Chapter 12 for cleanup information.)

If you're part of a household where someone else does most of the cooking, ask where various items are kept. You'll be surprised at all that they have around (and where it's all kept).

Never Cooked Before/Gotta Cook Now™   23

Dishes, serving pieces, and flatware

Once food has been prepared, you've got to eat it off something, which leads to dishes and flatware. A good beginning supply would include a plate, the aforementioned knife, fork, spoon; and a mug, or cup and saucer. You might also want:

4 dinner plates;

4 salad plates (can double as bread & butter dishes);

4 bowls (for soup, chili, salad, dessert);

4 cups;

4 saucers;

4 mugs (particularly if you are of the "saucers are a waste of time" school of life);

4 juice glasses (4 to 6 ounce capacity);

4 tumblers (8 to 12 ounce capacity);

4 beer glasses (admittedly optional, if you're of the "whaddaya mean? it's already in a can," school of life);

4 on-the-rocks or "old-fashioned" glasses;

4 all purpose wine glasses;

2 serving dishes, one flat, one with a raised rim;

4 dinner knives;

4 dinner forks;

4 salad forks;

4 soup spoons;

4 teaspoons;

2 serving spoons;

1 serving fork;

1 butter spreader;

1 butter dish;

1 salt shaker;

1 pepper shaker;

2 dish cloths;

4 dish towels;

1 plastic cutting board;

6 cloth napkins. One for each person. One for the bread basket (line the bread basket with it, put the bread in, and flip the corners over the top to keep the bread warm) and one extra;

1 box decent quality paper napkins;

2 rolls paper towels--one to use, and one spare;

1 tablecloth, might be a good idea to buy it to match the cloth napkins; (polyester/cotton blend, no ironing required, wash and wear type is highly recommended); these are great! Use them, toss in washing machine and dryer, fold them and put them away (or back on the table) without ironing.

if you can afford it, a second tablecloth and set of napkins is a really good idea;

one inexpensive straw-type basket, for bread (line with cloth napkin);

one trivet, or "hot plate" for hot dishes or pans. If no trivet, fold a dish towel or two and place under hot item; 1 four-sided, hollow-centered grater, with top handle, for grating carrots, bread crumbs, cheeses and similar items.

2 candlesticks and a few candles. If you're watching the budget, get a couple of inexpensive votive candles.

Why four of so many items? Because sometimes (if you're single) it's fun to have dinner with a friend. And sometimes (if you're part of a couple) it's fun to have dinner with another couple. And sometimes (no matter what your social situation) you might want to have some friends over to watch a game, or to play cards. And sometimes family shows up and it's, well, *politic* to offer them a little something and serve it in a manner that is approximately civilized. That's why. But you already knew that or you wouldn't be reading this.

A good many stores sell 50 or 54 piece sets that contain a lot of the items listed above. Or you can buy them separately or in subsets. Again, don't hesitate to go into the second-hand market if funds are tight. You'd be amazed at the things you can find really cheap at thrift stores, garage sales, and estate sales.

All right, you've assembled the fixtures, tools and equipment. You've placed them on the playing field, your kitchen. Now to get the moves down. We introduce you to:

Handy Kitchen Terms

Actually, the subhead is a bit of a misnomer, since this section also includes *unhandy* kitchen terms. However, the object remains the same: to explain the main words commonly used in cookery.

bake: to cook in an oven in a baking dish or pan;

blanch: to bring to a quick boil, then remove from heat;

boil: to immerse in water and heat until bubbles continuously form on the bottom of the liquid and rise to the top, where they burst. This condition is known as a full, rolling boil

braise: to cook in an oven, usually in liquid

broil: to cook over or under open flame or heat

chill: to take an object from room temperature to cooler than room temperature, usually by refrigerating, or placing in an ice bucket

chop: to cut into small pieces

cool: to take an object from above room temperature to room temperature

dice: to cut into pieces about 1/2 inch x 1/2 inch

fry: to cook in oil or fat in an open pan or vessel

grill: to cook on a flat, hot surface; or to cook over open flame on a series of bars, or grate.

mince: to chop into very small pieces, smaller than 1/4 inch

poach: to cook in liquid that is simmering, but not boiling. Often used for eggs, fish or poultry.

roast: to cook over a raised rack, in an roasting pan, in dry heat (usually an oven). Can also refer to cooking over an open fire, on a spit.

saute: to fry in a small amount of fat, usually over low or medium heat.

scald: to heat a liquid to a high temperature, until small bubbles form around the edges of the saucepan or heating vessel, but not as hot as boiling.

shred: a method of obtaining small, thin slivers of a food, often by using a grater or shredder; certain kinds of shredding can also be done with a knife. Food that has been shredded is usually in pieces that are somewhat longer and thinner than food that has been minced.

simmer: to cook in water that is hot but below the boiling point

slice: to cut thinner pieces from a large object, such as a loaf of bread or cut of meat; to divide an object, such as a pie or cake, into smaller pieces by cutting it with a knife.

steam: to cook placed on a rack inside a closed pot or vessel in which water has been heated to boiling, so that the steam released cooks the food. Usually, the food is not brought into contact with the boiling water when food is steamed

stir-fry: to fry quickly, over high heat, while stirring the items that are frying. Stir frying is often done in a slope-sided pan called a *wok*, but may also be done in a skillet

toast: to cook the surface of food by placing it close to a source of heat, such as direct flame or an electric heating element which has been brought to high temperature.

warm up: to bring an object from room temperature or below to a temperature that is warm or hot. Often used to describe the reheating of leftovers.

wok: a slope sided metal pan, used for stir-frying.

Weights and Measures

It is useful to get acquainted with measurements, or what equals what. Quantities for most ingredients used in North American recipes are expressed in the ounce and pound system for solids and in cups, pints and quarts for liquids. Some metric measurements are thrown in, since many international recipes are written for metric measurements.

Let's move from small to large. Ready? Okay.

pinch: in dry measurement, a pinch of something, usually a seasoning, herb, or spice, is what you can hold between your thumb and forefinger.

1/8 tsp.: this is generally the smallest size measured quantity used in cooking. Many measuring spoon sets will include the 1/8 teaspoon size as the smallest measuring spoon in the set. This measurement is generally larger than a pinch.

dash: eight drops of liquid.

1/4 tsp.: the 1/4 and 1/2 tsp. sizes are other common less-than teaspoon measurements.

1/2 tsp. See above.

1 teaspoon (tsp.) the teaspoon or tsp. is a common measurement for dry and for wet ingredients. A tsp. = about 1/6 of an ounce, liquid, or about five milliliters.

1 tablespoon (Tbs.): the tablespoon, abbreviated as Tbs., equals 3 teaspoons. In liquid measure, 1 tablespoon is 1/2 ounce.

1 ounce: two tablespoons (Tbs.) An ounce is generally expressed in the metric system as 28 grams or 28 milliliters liquid measure.

1/4 cup: Four tablespoons (Tbs.) = 1/4 cup. In liquid measure, 1/4 cup = 2 ounces.

1/2 cup: Eight tablespoons (Tbs.) = 1/2 cup. And 1/cup is four ounces. Four ounces = 1/4 pound, in solid measurements, and 1/8 quart, in liquid measure. One stick of butter = 1/2 cup of melted butter.

3/4 cup: Twelve Tbs. = 3/4 cup.

1 cup: Sixteen Tbs. = 1 cup. A cup is eight ounces. Some other

convenient things to remember: two sticks of butter equal one cup of melted butter.

1 pound: In dry measure, 16 ounces. or about 454 grams.

Meat, fruit, breads, coffee, lots of other items, are sold by the pound. Butter is more tricky. It is sold by the pound, but as you know, butter melts easily, and is often found in liquid form. Four sticks of butter comprise a pound; melted, four sticks of butter make up two liquid cups. Two sticks of butter, melted, equal one cup; and one stick of butter equals one half cup.

1 pint: Two cups = sixteen ounces. In dry measure, 16 ounces equal one pound, and roughly, one pound of dry measure equals one pint of liquid measure but one seldom hears of a pound of tomato juice" or a "pint of bread."

1 kilogram, or "kilo:" a metric measurement for dry weight.1 kilogram,or 1,000 grams = approximately 2.2 pounds. Recipes written for both the metric and U.S. systems usually equate one pound with 500 grams (1/2 kilo).

1 liter: A metric measurement for liquids. 1 liter is 1,000 milliliters. Generally, in cookbooks that are written for both metric and English systems of measurement, 250 milliliters are expressed as eight ounces, or one cup. A liter is about 33.4 ounces, or a little more than a quart.

1 quart: Two pints, or four cups, or 32 ounces, or about 60 milliliters.That's right--a quart weighs approximately two pounds, but since quarts are liquid measures and pounds are dry measures, very few people refer to two quarts of bread" or "two pounds of milk."

1 gallon: Four quarts, or 16 cups, or 128 fluid ounces, or about 3.84 liters.

Presentation is everything, Part I

How food is presented is important and affects the way the diner perceives the meal. Back when, there was a guy in school who had the good fortune to date a girl who was a few years older. She was beautiful, had a great personality, and was very poor.

Well, part of her poise and personality was the way she served-- food? No, she was too poor to serve food. She served black coffee. But she served that coffee as if it were a banquet. She would lay each place with a napkin, spoon, cup and saucer, and very elegantly pour the coffee from a battered old pot.

The care with which she set the table, the manner in which she held the pot, and the energy she invested in the ceremony made the guest (this guy) seem *important,* and made the coffee service seem quite dignified. He married her of course. So, it's not what you serve, it's the way that you serve it, to paraphrase the song. Below is one of the the most popular ways to set a table in most of North America.

Setting the table

   The plate is in front of the diner, fork on left, knife facing the plate, blade in, on the right. The teaspoon is to the right of the knife. Water and wine glasses go at the tip of the knife. Later, the glasses will be replaced by a cup and saucer, with the cup handle facing the right.

Use the outside utensils first

   If there is a salad fork, it is placed to the left, of the dinner fork, unless the salad is to be served after dinner. In other words, the fork to be used first is placed on the outside. If you're using a bread and butter plate, it should go on the left above the forks. If you're using individual butter spreaders, place each one across the top of the bread and butter plate, handle to the right.

Napkins

The napkin can be placed to the left of the forks, or, if you wish, directly on the plate. At the beginning of the meal, each diner places the napkin in his or her lap.

Add some "pizzazz" with candles

As mentioned previously, candles add a touch of elegance and are very flattering. We've all seen movies (or maybe been to such places) where little bistros have candles stuck in old wine bottles and somehow, romance blossoms at each table. You can use an old chianti bottle to hold a candle to illuminate casual dining. You can find candles, candle holders and candlesticks in all price ranges.

Add color with flowers

Flowers add color. You might want to think about keeping the height of the flowers low, so the diners can talk to one another. Sometimes its fun to put a single rose on its side somewhere on the table, or put a small bouquet at each plate.

Centerpieces

Centerpieces are items or arrangements placed in the middle of the table as focal points. They are limited only to the extent of your imagination. Try small stones for a striking minimalist effect; or ribbons and helium balloons on festive occasions. A neighbor used a dozen or so limes and lemons and an orange or two in a bowl as a fairly striking centerpiece. He made lemonade afterwards.

Holidays

For the Fourth of July use a small American flag placed in the center of the table. At holidays, try objects or decorations that relate to the holiday, such as glass ornaments at Yuletide, or use your imagination.

Valentines Day

For example, try a bowl of red candy hearts for Valentine's Day; red roses are always popular on February 14 as "flower of the day." Other good colors for this day are red and white.

July 4th

Try using red, white and blue decorations for the Fourth of July; decorations can be specifically patriotic or simply follow a red white and blue scheme. Ice cream with blueberries and strawberries picks up the holiday theme.

Halloween

Small pumpkins or ghost figures work well for Halloween; orange flowers like chrysanthemums go well with the decor.

Autumn dinner

Pick out some harvest-themed objects, such as Indian corn, nuts, or fall flowers as decorations for an Autumn dinner.

Thanksgiving

The Thanksgiving holiday carries the Autumn motif forward, but has specific items such as small items commemorating the Pilgrims and other early settlers that are often displayed at the table.

End of year holidays

The holidays celebrated at the end of the calendar year-- Christmas, Hanukkah, Kwanza, have traditional colors: green and red for Christmas; blue and silver for Hanukkah; and black, green and red for Kwanza. Often homes and tables are decorated for these holidays.

New Year's Eve

New Year's Eve is celebrated with elaborate table decorations as well. For the New Year, guests are sometimes given hats, noisemakers, and whistles.

Suggestions

Home and food magazines are full of suggestions for table decorations. Pick up a magazine (or flip through one at a newsstand) for additional ideas. Check out the China and tableware displays in kitchen stores, home stores, and department stores.

Actually, possibilities for table decoration are virtually unlimited, and entire books have been written about the subject. There will be more presentation tips at strategic places throughout the book.

Chapter Two

Stocking Up

LOOKING around your kitchen, maybe no one is going to confuse it with "Ye Olde Harvest Feaste." Don't let that stop you. Move in the direction of Ye Olde Harvest Feaste by stocking the old larder.

Taking inventory

What's in your kitchen now? If the answer is "nothing," life is simple. Just follow the five week plan outlined below. But if there are items in your pantry that you intend to use, adjust the plan to your existing stockpile of foods.

The five week plan

This Stocking Up list is broken down into five weeks, just as the menus are divided into five one week periods, and this chapter covers the first week, or Week One. The first week presents the most basic shopping list, a list of items that should always be around (the "always theres") and Chapter Two, covering menus and recipes for Week One, contains the simplest menus. Each week, the shopping lists become more extensive and the menus become more varied in ingredients and more complex, reflecting the fact that you'll be getting more skilled.

This strategy also permits you to spread the purchase of herbs and spices, over the entire five-week period. See **About Herbs and Spices** at the end of this chapter. Spices and herbs can be expensive, so this method is a bit easier on the wallet than buying everything at once. But, hey--if you have the money, and you want to get all these supplies up front, by all means go for it.

The Always Theres™

Here are some items you will want to have "always there." This is a short list of some of the kinds of foodstuffs and supplies you might want to keep around on a fairly constant basis:

apples, fresh
applesauce, canned or jarred
artichokes, marinated, in jar

baking mix or biscuit mix
baking powder (double acting)
baking soda
beans, dried
beans, canned
bullion, canned or cubes (or both--cans are faster to use)
butter

chicken or turkey, canned
catsup (or ketchup)

cereals (cold)
cereals (hot)
chocolate, semi-sweet (one ounce squares for baking)
chocolate, unsweetened (one ounce squares for baking)
cinnamon
cheese for eating (cheddar, cream, Swiss, etc.)
cheese for cooking (mozzarella, Parmesan, etc.)
coffee, ground
coffee, instant
cocoa powder
cooking oil
corn starch

crackers

eggs

fish, canned (salmon, tuna)
fruit, fresh (such as melons, grapefruit, pears)
fruit juices, fresh, canned, or frozen

garlic, fresh
garlic, powdered (optional)

ham or other canned luncheon meat

jam, jelly or preserves (such as strawberry jam)

mayonnaise
milk, condensed, canned
milk, evaporated, canned
milk, fresh
milk, powdered
mustard, prepared or dry, or both

onion, fresh, or flakes, or both

paper towels
paper napkins
pasta
peppers, bell (sweet peppers, red, green, or other colors)
pepper, black, ground
pepper, red (hot pepper)

raisins or other dried fruit

salt, iodized
soups (canned or dry mix)
sugar, brown, and sugar, white
shortening

tea bags

The Always Theres™ Lead to the "There's Always"

If you've got some things on hand at all times (the Always Theres™) you won't likely be hungry, because when some things are on hand at all times, one can revert to the "There's Always"-- as in "There's always some elbow macaroni and canned tuna--we can do a quick casserole."

Week One

Since food is organized by category in super markets, shopping is easier if you organize your shopping list by those same categories. The shopping lists for this book are organized in the same manner.

When you start organizing your own shopping lists, one system you might try is organizing the list the way your local market is physically laid out. For example, the first thing you see on entering the store is produce, put the produce items at the beginning of your list.

By the way, some of the items you'll be buying this week will not be used up right away. Make them part of your Always Theres™ stash.

Fresh foods

These foods generally do not keep well after a certain number of days have passed, and they need to be purchased frequently. Many fresh foods, and some staples, contain expiration dates.

About Expiration Dates

These are the little "best when purchased by" or "use before" dates that appear on milk, butter, cheese, dry cereal, bread, and lots of other items. Generally, the further into the future the expiration date is, the better for you. Baked goods and fresh dairy products, such as milk, usually stay fresh for a limited time, such as a week or so. Items like butter and eggs last a bit longer.

Bacon typically can be stored for a couple of weeks. Fresh beef and pork should be cooked within two days; and fresh fish and poultry should be cooked as soon as possible; these shouldn't be kept at home in the refrigerator longer than two days, although they can be frozen, and thawed and cooked later. Cereal and baking mix sometimes can be kept for periods up to a year. Be sure to consult labels on packages for advice on how long the product will remain fresh.

Dairy products

Virtually all dairy products need refrigeration. Many dairy products are high in fat; but there are low fat and non-fat alternatives exist. Some low-fat alternatives are listed below.

Milk. How much? You decide. How much are you drinking now? Buy about that much. If you aren't drinking any, buy one quart of 2% milk. Always check the expiration date. Buy the milk that has the expiration date that is the furthest into the future.

Low-fat alternative: you can get milk with 1% butterfat, or 1/2% butterfat, or skim milk at many stores.

Eggs. One dozen, large. Ever bought eggs before? If so, you know to open the carton and check to make certain there are no cracked eggs; check the expiration date, as well. Buy the eggs with the latest expiration date. These simple steps save much grief.

Low-fat alternative: low fat or fat free egg substitutes are available in many super markets.

Butter or margarine. These items are largely interchangeable. Generally, butter is more expensive and tastes better. But there are lots of good margarine brands on the market. If you're on a really tight budget, there are some very low-priced margarines available, and while they aren't butter, they really aren't bad. One of the benefits of regular (not low-fat) butter/margarine is that it can be used in cooking and baking, as well as in general table spread duty (toast, baked potatoes, you name it).

Low-fat alternatives: There are many low fat versions of margarine and butter blends available. Check the labels.

Heads up: some low fat margarines or butters can't be used in cooking or baking because of their high water content--make certain to read the label.

Cheese. This week, buy one pound of single sliced process cheese, Swiss or American. Buy four ounces of shredded cheese. You might vary the type from week to week. If you purchased American (cheddar) slices, you might want to buy shredded mozzarella (a softer, white cheese) later. What if you plan to serve cheese as an appetizer or for snacking? Then buy a chunk of your favorite non-process cheese, the kind the grocer or deli person cuts from a wheel or block of cheese.

Low-fat alternative: There are several low-fat and no-fat cheeses or cheese products on the market.

Cream cheese, one eight-ounce block: (Lowfat versions are available.) Good for sandwiches and appetizers.

Low-fat alternative: There are low fat and fat free cream cheeses and sour creams available in many stores (see below).

Whipping cream: one half-pint.

Sour cream. One sixteen ounce container.

Meat and Fish

Hamburger: two pounds. Fat varies in ground beef. The cheaper the hamburger, the more fat. Ground chuck is a good compromise.

Chicken: One cut up fryer, about 2.5 to 3 pounds;

Tip: poultry should be used within a day or two of purchase; if planning to use later than second day after purchase, store the poultry in the freezer and defrost before cooking.

Low-fat alternative: Removing the skin from chicken before cooking is a good way to reduce fat.

Fish, filet. Try orange roughy, flounder, sole, or other sort of white ocean fish. A serving of fresh fish should be about eight ounces per person, uncooked. Most fish shrinks in cooking.

Fish, salmon. Purchase about 8 ounces to 1 pound of salmon. Salmon is sold in steaks (containing bones) and filets, which have been boned. It is not difficult to remove the bones, but you may prefer to have the fish merchant do this for you. Salmon is great for leftovers.

Ham steaks, 2, about 1 pound;

Hot dogs, one pound. There are many types and varieties of franks on the market. Beef-pork mixture may be one of the most common; if you want lower fat, try some of the turkey franks. Either type will work in these recipes. So will all beef. You'll need at least eight individual hot dogs (two meals out of these babies this week);

Tip: It's always a good idea to read the ingredients label. It's especially important to read the ingredients labels on hot dogs and sausage packages, since there are so many types on the market and they are made of so many varieties of meat.

Bacon, sliced, one pound. Bacon is a very versatile meat, in that it can be used to enhance the flavor of other foods, provides a lot of taste and textural contrast, and yields bacon fat when cooked. The bacon fat can be used to fry other foods. (Ask any camper.);

Pork chops, 4, about 1 pound;

Steaks, T-bone, Delmonico, New York Strip, or filet, about six ounces to 1/2 pound for each person you are planning to serve.

Produce

Apples, three pounds. There are many varieties of apples on the market. This week, pick a kind that's red, like Paula Red, Macintosh, Northern Spy, Ida Red, Cortland, Jonathan or Winesap. When purchasing apples, many people buy the red Delicious variety, but some find them to be somewhat less flavorful than other varieties. (The red Delicious variety are exceptionally pretty, though, if you're doing a centerpiece or a display for "Ye Olde Harvest Feaste.")

Bananas, one bunch, say four or five. Chose bananas that are yellow, but not too green (under ripe) nor too brown (overripe). Remember bananas will continue to ripen in your kitchen. Bananas do not need refrigeration

Carrots, one pound. If you have the means, buy them prewashed and peeled; if not, buy them as they come from the farm, in the one pound bag, and wash and peel them yourself.

Celery, one bunch. A bunch of celery is also called a "stalk." A single celery stem is called a "rib." Celery is another of those "utility player" foods. It adds flavor and texture to all kinds of recipes, and makes a great snack, appetizer, and even a stand-alone cooked vegetable (honest).

Lemon, one medium. Lemons are a great enhancer for other foods. Good sliced, in iced tea. Good cut into sections and squeezed on broccoli or fish. Good mixed with oil, for salad dressing. And the yellow part of the rind, known as the "zest" can be used for flavoring. Squeezed and mixed with water and sugar, lemons make lemonade, a terrific beverage.

Lettuce, one head. Since you're just getting started, buy a head of iceberg or "head" lettuce. It's the kind found on fast food burgers and budget steak house salad bars. Not terribly flavorful, but crunchy and good to practice on. If you're feeling adventuresome, buy two heads of lettuce and make the second one Romaine.

Romaine lettuce is looser, more rectangular, and darker green. There are other good varieties of lettuce, including Boston, and oak leaf lettuce.

Onions, three pounds. Yellow cooking onions are fine, and frequently the least expensive; green onions (scallions) add color and sharpness; purple onions are good in salads.

Vidalia onions are highly regarded for their mild flavor. Scallions and leeks are types of onions, and can be substituted for regular onions in a pinch.

Tip: Carrots, celery and onions are the "standout stewards" of the "serious chef." In addition to serving as an ingredient or a garnish, each of these can be a stand-alone item, and can be served raw or cooked, hot, cold, or at room temperature.

Many recipes begin with green onions, or scallions as they are also known. They can be used as a *crudite* (cold vegetables, chopped or sliced, and served as an appetizer or *hors d'ouevre*. Carrots add color and texture to lots of different dishes and also make a great cooked vegetable, as well as a great addition to a *crudite* platter. Celery adds depth and flavor of its own to soups, stews, and salads and it, too, is a terrific snack item.

You will notice that the orange of carrots, the white, dark green or purple found in onions, and the pale green of the celery also provide good color contrast to one another and when used with other foods. This is why onions, carrots and celery are used so often in salads, relish trays, and as garnishes.

Garlic, one head. Traditionally, heads of garlic are sold in the produce department; each head has many individual cloves. "Fresh" garlic has already been dried at the farm and will keep for a number of weeks in a cool dry place. Or try garlic powder, sold in jars in the herbs and spices section of the market. Stay away from garlic salt.

Heads up: a round "bunch" of garlic is called a "head" of garlic. A section of garlic from the head is called a "clove" of garlic. Garlic and ground cloves, the aromatic spice used in baking, have nothing to do with one another.

Oranges, five or six. Navel oranges don't have seeds and taste good.

Parsley, one bunch. Parsley comes in two varieties: curly or flat (Italian). Many people find curly parsley to be more versatile, and look better, but both taste fine; use parsley as a garnish, a vegetable and an herb. It keeps in the refrigerator about a week.

Potatoes: five pounds. Russet potatoes are a good all-purpose potato. "Idaho" and "Maine" potatoes are russets. These are good for baking, frying and boiling; Smaller redskin potatoes are very good boiled, steamed, and in salads. A good yellow-fleshed potato is the Yukon gold variety.

Green bell peppers: two, medium. Bell peppers are sweet, not hot, as chiles and jalapenos can be. Bell peppers are another very useful vegetable. You can eat them uncooked, or fry, boil, broil, or roast them; they can be stuffed with a wide variety of ingredients, and used as garnishes or containers for other foods. Make certain the ones you purchase are crisp and firm.

Bell peppers come in many colors, including red, yellow, purple, orange and white, as well as green. The red bell peppers are more mature than the green, and somewhat sweeter. They add flavor and color to many dishes. Different colors add "eye appeal" to foods.

Strawberries: one pint. Generally, fresh strawberries are superior to frozen. They should be used fairly promptly. If you are a big fruit eater, buy a quart of strawberries instead of a pint;

Fresh tomatoes: two or three, medium.

Tip: Wash fruits and vegetables just before using them, unless you strip off the protective peel, as with bananas and oranges.

Frozen (or fresh) products

Fruit juice: Your call. It is possible to purchase fruit juices in a number of varieties and degrees of freshness. Some markets sell fresh squeezed orange and grapefruit juices.

Tight budget? Buy a couple of six ounce cans of frozen concentrated orange or grapefruit juice. Follow package directions and have some each morning. If you're able to do so, buy a couple of varieties of juice (orange and apple; or cranberry/something and grape. You get the idea);

Peas, frozen: Get the 16 ounce bag and shake out as many as you need for a given meal. Frozen peas and other vegetables are sold in boxes or bags The bag packaging allows flexibility, since the bag can be re-closed and placed back in the freezer. That way, what isn't cooked is available for another day.

Many folks say fresh peas are better than frozen. Others say that not only are frozen peas as good as fresh, they're actually *better*, since they were picked and frozen at peak of freshness. Since frozen peas are a *lot* less trouble than fresh, and taste *way* better than canned, they look like the way to go. You might want a can of peas in your "Always there" larder, as a backup. Go with whatever works for you.

Green beans: frozen. Follow same procedure as for peas;

Corn: frozen, cut into kernels. Same procedure as peas and green beans;

Broccoli: frozen, or fresh. Get the sixteen ounce bag of frozen broccoli cuts or the ten ounce box. You can also use fresh broccoli. Fresh broccoli is fairly easy to prepare, and it can also be used uncooked, for salads or *hors d'oeuvres*. If purchasing fresh broccoli, look for firm green heads.

Waffles: frozen. Get a dozen or so. Prepare them in your toaster or toaster oven. No toaster? You can bake these in the oven, too; use a cookie sheet, place the waffles on the cookie sheet and place in 350° F. oven; turn once when top is done.

Staples

Foods that keep without refrigeration for a long time are sometimes referred to as staples. They include dry foods, such as flour and rice; durable baked goods, such as crackers; certain liquids, such as oils and syrups; spices and herbs; and canned items. Most canned foods have been cooked at very high temperatures and need only be heated to be ready to eat, or can be eaten without additional cooking. Other staples include prepared foods, such as dry cereal, that will keep for a number of weeks or months. Be sure to read package labels about storage.

Canned foods

Baked beans, two cans 15 ounces each. Usually these beans are sold in tomato sauce, sometimes with a bit of pork, and labeled as "pork and beans"--they go really well with franks, burgers, ribs, and just about anything you can barbecue; they're not bad with ham, either. Dress them up by adding chopped onion, bacon, brown sugar, or catsup.

Vegetarian alternative: Baked beans are also available in vegetarian varieties.

Kidney beans, one can, 15 ounce size. Great in chili, with rice, or in three bean salad.

White beans, one can, 15 ounce size. These are sometimes called Navy, Great Northern, or canellini beans. Excellent in many dishes, hot and cold.

Fish, salmon, one can (if you're not buying fresh salmon). Use the seven ounce size for one or two persons, or the 15 ounce size can for three or four people.

Fish, tuna, two cans 6.5 to 7 ounces each. Tuna comes in several quality levels, with solid white albacore at the top of the ladder, and chunk dark tuna at the bottom. Tuna is also available packed in several liquids, such as vegetable broth, oil, or spring water.

Chunk light is okay if you're watching your budget. Packed in spring water is the way to go if you're watching your waist. Packed in oil is fine if you're going to make a Nicoise salad.

Peanut butter: one jar. What size? Depends on how much you like peanut butter. But get a half pound, at least. At super markets, peanut butter seems to be sold in 12-ounce and 18 ounce sizes, as well as larger sizes. Some people keep peanut butter in the refrigerator after opening, some people don't. If you don't eat lots of peanut butter, the refrigerator is the place to store it.

Soup: two or three cans cream of mushroom (or any other "cream of" flavor you like) condensed soup.

Low-fat or low salt alternatives: some condensed soups are available in low-fat versions; and there are condensed soups on the market with a lower salt content.

Tip: Remember this: condensed soups are the beginning cook's special friend. No, they don't taste as good as fresh. Yes, you can make your own mushroom soup with some beef stock, fresh mushrooms, butter, a bit of onion, and some cream, mince the onions, wash the mushrooms, stir constantly, don't let the cream burn, add just the right seasoning, garnish with red pepper curls-- *but*--condensed soup is fast and versatile; it can be manipulated to make either soup or sauce; and it is invaluable in certain casseroles or other baked dishes. You will probably want to make your own mushroom soup from scratch at the end of this book, not the beginning.

Jam or jelly: one jar. Try strawberry for openers. Jams and preserves have more fruit, and more intense flavor, but are used in the same way. Second jar? Try grape jam or orange marmalade.

Mayonnaise, one pint, one jar.

Low-fat alternative: mayonnaise is also sold in low fat and nonfat versions. Read the label on the jar for details.

Molasses: unsulphured, one jar.

Mustard: one jar, perhaps five or six ounces. Mustard that comes in jars and is ready to spread is called "prepared" mustard. You will find many varieties of mustard on the shelves. Dijon is sharper. Bright yellow mustards are generally milder. Chinese mustard is extremely hot. Powdered mustard, which needs to be mixed with water before use, is optional. You decide.

Oil, olive: 1 pint or one-half liter jar, for salads and frying. If you have the means and the inclination, you may want to buy a second jar of a different kind of oil, such as corn oil or soybean oil. Corn oil is lighter in flavor than olive oil.

Peaches: sliced, or halves, one can. Look for yellow cling variety. The sixteen ounce size will serve four people;

Tip: if fresh peaches are available in the marketplace, and you intend to use them fairly quickly, buy fresh peaches instead of canned. Unlike apples, fresh peaches cannot be stored for long periods of time and are not always available in stores.

Potatoes: sliced or whole, one can. A great time saver when you are in need of a starch and don't have time to prepare one from scratch. This can of potatoes is for your "Always There™" stockpile. If you use a lot of potatoes, and don't have much time, you may want to buy more than one can.

Sliced pimentos: small jar (2 ounce or 4 ounce size) These are for adding color to a dish or to be used as a garnish.;

Salad dressing: some folks swear by salad dressings made from scratch. Others use only bottled dressing. It's perfectly acceptable to use either, depending upon how much time you have. Bottled dressing, tastes fine and saves lots of time. Try French or ranch. Be sure to refrigerate the dressing after opening.

Tomatoes: whole or crushed, 28 ounces, one can. Indispensable for spaghetti sauce.

Tomato sauce: 8 ounces, two or three cans. Use in meals you prepare from scratch; also good for meat loaf, green beans, and leftovers.

Tomato juice: 46 ounces, one can.

Vinegar: 16 ounces, one bottle. Get distilled white vinegar. Later on, try flavored vinegars.

Dried foods

Baking mix or biscuit mix: These come in sizes that vary. For example, 40 ounces (2 and one-half pounds) or fifty-four ounces (3 pounds, six ounces). Exactly why, it is difficult to say. You should definitely comparison shop for this item, because the leading brand is significantly more expensive than other brands, and there is very little difference in the product. Baking mix is flour with added fat and leavening. It makes life easier and therefore it is really useful.

Basil: one jar of dried chopped basil; basil is an aromatic herb, used with sauces and salads. Although used fresh or dried, dried is more common, and fresh basil is hard to locate in the winter;

Beans, dried: one pound. Navy beans, pinto beans, or red kidney beans will do. These require an overnight soak (or a business day soak) before cooking. Be sure to change the water after soaking and before cooking. If you don't think that sort of preparation fits in with your lifestyle, canned beans will do just fine;

Black pepper: ground. One, two, or four ounce metal box. This is a good all around spice. Using a pepper mill and grinding whole black peppercorns produces pepper that is fresher with better flavor, but ground black pepper is fine. See the **About Herbs and Spices** at the end of this chapter for a full list of herbs and spices, and the weeks to purchase them.

Brownie mix: Or blondie mix. One box. "Blondies" are brownies without the chocolate; sometimes they have a butterscotch flavor. If you intend to make brownies from scratch, be sure you have all the ingredients called for in the recipe on p. 235.

Cereal: dry, ready-to-eat, one box. Can't decide? Most people will eat corn flakes. Buy the variety you enjoy most; if it fits the budget, buy a second, made from a different grain (or grains).

Cheese: grated Parmesan, or Romano, or a blend of the two. If you live in a neighborhood with an Italian store, pass up the round can and get the real thing, which you can grate yourself, or have them grate it for you. Keep freshly grated cheese it in a tightly sealed container.

Canned grated Italian cheeses sometimes have preservatives added and do not require refrigeration; so read the label to see if the product you are buying should or should not be refrigerated. The fresh versions do require refrigeration.

Cinnamon: four ounces, ground. Cinnamon is really good for baking and desserts; it is also used in some chili recipes.

Oregano: one jar of dried chopped oregano. Used in soups, sauces, salads, and to flavor meats.

Rice: one one-pound bag of brown or white rice. Brown rice takes longer to cook, has a nuttier flavor, and contains more fiber. White rice is slightly more bland. Budget permitting, buy both.

Tip--Instant or "quick" rice may work for you. Instant rice is rice that has been partially precooked, and is ready in a short time. Directions vary, so check those on the box you purchase.

Salt: one pound, *iodized*. Iodine is a necessary nutrient and is naturally occurring in salt. Some salt is sold with the iodine removed. Get the iodized type unless you are allergic to iodine.

Soup mix: dry, onion, one two-envelope box. Great for soup, for mixing with sour cream or yogurt as a dip.

Sugar: white, granulated. One four pound (or two kilo) bag. (A kilo is 2.2 pounds.)

Baked Goods

Hamburger buns: one bag. These usually contain six or eight buns. They freeze well, so you may want to use half and freeze the rest.

Bread: one pound loaf. Try rye, or another variety. You can vary the type from week to week. If you are cooking for one or two, bread is easy to freeze, and also keeps well in the refrigerator.

Chips: one bag potato or corn chips (if you're a chip eater).

Cookies: one box (if you're a cookie eater). Remember that this book has a number of cookie recipes.

Crackers: one or two boxes. If you're buying just one box, get an all purpose cracker. These are good with soup, cheeses, fruit, as a base for other munchies, or simply by themselves.

Beverages

Beverages include coffee and tea, which are found in the dried foods list, milk, found in the dairy foods list, and fruit juice, found in the frozen foods and canned foods lists. Beverages also include "pop" or carbonated beverages, usually sold in glass or plastic bottles, or in cans; beer, sold in glass or plastic bottles, or in cans; wines, usually sold in glass bottles; as well as still (non-carbonated) or sparking (carbonated or naturally effervescent) mineral waters, usually sold in glass bottles.

About Herbs and Spices

The herbs and spices used in this book's recipes are discussed below, along with suggested weeks for purchasing them. If you can afford it, buy all of them at once. There are many kinds and types of herbs and spices besides those used in this book. Some herbs, like celery, garlic, and parsley are also used as vegetables. Try both fresh and dried versions of some of these herbs. Some of the items listed below are used so frequently that they are part of the Always Theres™ discussed in the first part of this chapter.

Herb and spice list

allspice, Week Four
basil, Week One.
bay leaf, Week Four
black pepper, ground, Week One
capers, Week Five
caraway seeds, Week Five
celery, Week One
chili peppers, (hot red peppers) ground, Week Two
chives, Week Four
cinnamon, Week One
cloves, Week Two
cumin, Week Five
curry powder, Week Four
dill, Week Two

garlic, Week One
ginger, Week Three
horseradish, prepared, Week Five
marjoram, Week Four
mustard, Week One
nutmeg, Week Two
oregano, Week One
paprika, Week Three
parsley, Week One
peppercorns, black, Week One
rosemary, Week Three
sage, Week Two
saffron, Week Five
thyme, Week Three
vanilla extract, Week Three

Week One

Basil. Sold dried and ground. Use in salads, pasta sauce or soups.

Black pepper. Sold ground, or in peppercorns.

Celery. Sold in the produce section.

Cinnamon. Used in baked goods. Buy the ground form.

Garlic. An Always There.™ Sold by the head in the produce section or powdered in the spice section. Avoid garlic salt.

Mustard, prepared. Sold in the condiment section. Dried mustard is sold in the spice section. There are many varieties of each.

Oregano. Sold ground. Use in salads, some baked dishes, sauces.

Parsley. Sold fresh in the produce section of the supermarket. Dried parsley is sold in the and spice section.

Week Two

Cloves, ground. Good in baking and with ham.

Dill weed. Sold dried or fresh. Use on fish, in salads, and dips.

Nutmeg. Excellent in baked goods. Sold in ground form.

Hot red pepper, ground. Use sparingly. Experiment with the many kinds of red or green chili peppers. Do not confuse "hot" red pepper, the spice, with sweet red bell peppers, a vegetable.

Sage. Terrific in sauces, salads, and with meats, such as pork.

Week Three

Ginger, ground. Used in baking and fish and meat dishes.

Paprika, ground. Adds mild pepper flavor and red color.

Rosemary, leaves. Excellent with potatoes, meats, soups.

Thyme, leaf. Good in stuffings and as a garnish.

Vanilla extract. Adds flavor to baked goods. Sold as a liquid.

Week Four

Allspice. Used in baking and stuffings.

Bay leaf. Use in soups and stews. Remove before serving.

Chives. Mild green onion-like herb. Sold dried.

Curry powder. A blend of many spices and herbs. Several varieties on the market. Used in Indian foods, rice and soups.

Marjoram. Use in salads, and with meats and fish.

Week Five

Capers. Good with fish, in salads, and as a garnish.

Caraway seeds. Used in baking, especially in rye breads.

Cumin. An ingredient of chili powder.

Fennel. The seeds are from the fennel plant, which resembles celery, and have a mild licorice flavor. The vegetable is found in markets on a seasonal basis, and is sometimes served braised.

Horseradish, prepared. Flavors beef, fish, and beets well. Sold in jars. Keep refrigerated.

Saffron. Mild flavor, bright yellow color for rice, oriental dishes. Saffron is fairly expensive, so use it sparingly.

Many other spices and herbs are used to flavor and preserve food. Indeed, entire books have been written on the subject. If you have the time and the interest, you may wish to visit one of the larger markets in your area to see what spices and herbs are available there, and to experiment with them. Most spice containers suggest uses for the particular spice within.

Different cuisines use a good deal of particular herbs and spices. For example, lemon grass, an herb with a slight lemony flavor, is frequently found in Thai cooking. Indian and Mexican cooking each use a large variety of hot chilis. Some Italian recipes call for nutmeg. Saffron is called for in Oriental dishes, and also in Spanish cooking, in recipes like *paella*. Scandinavian cooking has many recipes that call for fresh or dried dill, or for cardamom.

Chapter Three

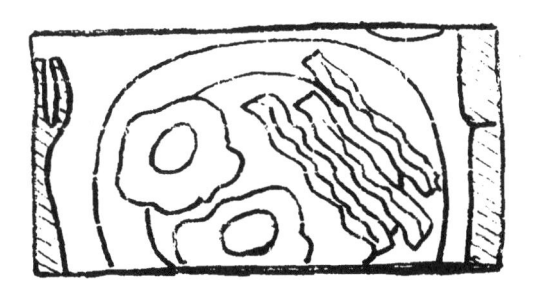

Menus and Recipes for Week One

YOU'VE equipped your kitchen, and gone out and bought some food. Now, to prepare, cook, present, serve, and eat it. Everyone knows someone who slams a frozen dinner into the microwave and eats it standing over the sink, but you're ready for something more.

Tip: you may find that it's a good idea to shop for foods more frequently than once a week, particularly if you are planning to eat a good deal of poultry or fish. These items should be used fairly quickly once they are purchased.

You'll find that the menus go from simple to complex, and contain a wider variety of ingredients as you move through them. The first recipes may well be for meals you already know how to prepare. If so, chalk it up to "the thrill of the familiar." If not, the early recipes are simple to provide initial success and the experience to take you into more complex meals.

These beginning menus use recipes that do not require a broad range of ingredients. As discussed in Chapter Two, that lets you acquire staples and spices over the five week period, instead of having to lay out a lot of cash all at once.

Now, everyone is aware that one month contains thirty-one days at most. However, there are **thirty-five** each of breakfast, lunch, snack, and dinner menus set forth in this book. to set out a five-week menu program. This provides flexibility, variety, and alternatives for folks who have allergies, or who never eat tuna fish, or who just can't abide winter squash.

Then, just for fun we throw in a few recipes for appetizers, for a dinner party, or for watching the game of the week; or whatever. The appetizers are usually found just before the menus for Saturday or Sunday dinners. They can be ganged together to make a selection for a great party.

Weekly Cycles

The menus and recipes are presented in five one-week cycles, since many folks like to do their marketing on a weekly basis. They run in the order of breakfast, lunch, snack, dinner, but you can bounce that around to suit your own needs. The weeks start on Monday, like business weeks, and end on Sundays.

Week One Menus

Monday

Breakfast: Cold cereal, milk, sliced banana, bread or toast, butter, jelly, or both; coffee, tea or other beverage, orange juice

Lunch: Grilled cheese and tomato sandwich, apple, iced tea, milk, or other beverage, small candy bar (optional)

Snack: Carrot sticks

Dinner: Meat loaf #1, baked potatoes, green beans, bread and butter, iced tea, Ice cream

Tuesday

Breakfast: Baked apples, toast, juice, coffee or tea.

Lunch: Tuna salad or tuna salad sandwiches, fresh pear, beverage, rolls (if no sandwiches), sliced peaches (optional)

Snack: Brownie (store bought or made with brownie mix) and beverage

Dinner: Ham steaks, peas, au gratin potatoes, green salad #1, beer bread, fresh strawberries, mineral water.

Wednesday

Breakfast: Scrambled eggs, bacon, potatoes, coffee or tea, toast, jelly, juice.

Lunch: Franks and beans, sliced tomatoes with vinaigrette dressing.

Snack: Green pepper rings, crackers, cola drink.

Dinner: American spaghetti, red sauce #I, green salad #II, garlic bread, red wine, coffee, and tira misu #I.

Alternate recipe: spaghetti carbonara.

Thursday

Breakfast: Waffles, syrup, butter, strawberries, juice, coffee or tea.

Lunch: Peanut butter and banana sandwich, carrot sticks, beverage, apple.

Snack: Cookies and beverage.

Dinner: Pork chop and rice casserole, bread and butter, coffee, vanilla ice cream.

Friday

Breakfast: Cold cereal with bananas or strawberries, juice, coffee, toast.

Lunch: Hamburgers on buns, ketchup, mustard, relish, onions, home fries, green beans, cola drink, ice cream, cookies.

Snack: Popcorn and small glass of juice.

Dinner: Tuna noodle casserole, broccoli, applesauce, drop biscuits, coffee, fresh strawberries.

Saturday

Breakfast: Pancakes, syrup, butter, orange slices, bacon, beverage.

Lunch: Chicken boullion, egg salad sandwich, cucumber slices, milk.

Snack: Apple, cheese wedge, hot tea.

Appetizer: Chips with onion dip

Dinner: Steaks, baked potatoes, corn, bread and butter, salad, red wine, lemon crisp cookies with ice cream.

Sunday

Breakfast: Waffles, sauteed apples and bananas, coffee or tea.

Lunch: Salmon rice salad, tomato slices, rye bread, cola drink.

Snack: Pretzel sticks, an orange, and iced tea.

Appetizer: Fresh vegetable (*crudites*) tray.

Dinner: Chicken artichoke bake, roasted potatoes and carrots, green salad I, corn bread and butter, white wine, ice cream.

Monday, Week One

Breakfast

Cold cereal, milk, sliced banana, bread or toast, butter or jelly or both, coffee, tea or other beverage, orange juice.

Light eating alternatives

Lighter eaters can eliminate the cereal or bread, and folks who are watching their weight can delete the butter and use sugarless all fruit spread instead of jelly or jam. You'll notice this breakfast can be made without any particular recipes, and is great for days when you are in a hurry and do not have time to cook. However, some folks can probably use a word or two on coffee and tea, the two "leading" breakfast hot beverages.

Coffee and Tea Basics

The fastest way to make coffee is to use instant coffee. Generally speaking, instant coffee is acceptable, but doesn't taste as good as perked coffee, and perked coffee is not as good as brewed coffee.

Instant coffee is available in powdered form, usually in glass jars and is fast and cheap. Add a cup of boiling hot water to a teaspoon of the powder, and zam! you've got a cup of coffee. Many folks think instant coffee lacks the full-bodied flavor of brewed coffee.

Perked coffee is coffee made in a percolator, a method that boils water, forces the boiled water up through a tube, and down over a basket full of ground coffee beans. If you have a percolator, by all means, use it. If you don't have one, don't buy one. Instead, buy a coffee brewer. There are many brands of coffee brewers on the market.

Brewed coffee is made in a coffee brewer. These are the ubiquitous coffee machines seen everywhere, and are generally regarded as making more flavorful coffee than percolators. Coffee brewers work by pouring water just below the boiling point over coffee which has been placed in a paper filter and put into a plastic basket. The basket fits beneath the hot water tap on the machine. The coffee falls into a carafe, which usually has an insulated handle. This is considered the best way to make regular "North American" coffee.

Many people seem to prefer coffee made with water that has not been boiled. Brewers heat the water to a high temperature, just below boiling, while percolators boil the water. Some folks say that the boiling water used in percolators does not bring out the best flavor of the coffee, but perked coffee is "hotter" for those who enjoy really hot coffee.

Tea. There are at least as many ways to make tea as there are to make coffee, although the machinery is less complicated. Basically, tea leaves or tea powder are placed into boiling water; or, boiling water is poured over tea leaves. Tea bags provide a way to mix tea leaves and water without leaving tea leaves in the cup. The longer the tea bag or leaves steep in the hot water, the stronger the tea is. You may want to start with a good all purpose tea, such as orange pekoe. There are many varieties of tea, including breakfast teas, and flavored teas. Many are quite good.

Numerous other types and varieties of coffees and teas exist. Experiment as you go along, until you find the varieties you prefer.

Both coffee and tea should be stored in closed containers until you are ready to brew them. Since coffee goes stale over time, it is useful to freeze any coffee you're not planning on using within a few weeks. Leftover coffee or leftover tea can be refrigerated and used for iced coffee or iced tea. Or iced tea or coffee may be made by pouring hot or cold tea or coffee over ice. Pouring hot beverages over ice causes the ice to melt very quickly, diluting the beverage. For this reason, tea or coffee that is to be iced is sometimes made stronger than when it is to be served hot.

Lunch

Grilled cheese and tomato sandwich on rye bread, an apple, iced tea, milk or other beverage. Dessert (optional): small candy bar.

Grilled cheese and tomato sandwich.

For each sandwich, you will need:
two slices rye bread.
butter or margarine.
Two slices American or Swiss cheese.
tomato slices.

Use a cast iron frying pan, or use a grill if you have one. Butter the two slices of bread on both sides. Place the buttered side of one slice face down and place cheese on the slice of bread, top with tomato slices, and place other slice of bread on top, buttered side out. Grill in frying pan until bread is done to the degree you prefer, then turn sandwich over, using pancake turner, and grill other side. Serves one. Multiply ingredients to provide more servings.

Toaster oven variation: don't butter the outsides of the sandwich, and toast in toaster oven, turning if your toaster oven only toasts on one side. Be neat, so the cheese doesn't drip out. If it does, clean the drip tray before you use the toaster oven again.

Snack

Carrot sticks. These are low in fat and taste pretty good.

Carrot sticks.

2 carrots

Wash and peel carrots, using a potato peeler. Cut lengthwise a few times, then cut into sticks about 3" long. The carrots will keep well in the refrigerator in a plastic sandwich bag. If you are preparing this snack a day or so in advance, the carrots will keep well in the refrigerator in a glass or jar of water. Serves one or two.

Dinner

Meat loaf, baked potatoes, green beans, bread and butter. Iced tea. Ice cream.

Baked potatoes.

Preheat oven to 350° F. Wash four medium sized potatoes, and use potato peeler or small knife to remove eyes, root tubers, or anything else on the potato you're not particularly interested in consuming. Put the potatoes on a baking sheet, or in an open baking dish and bake for about one hour. Serves four.

Microwave version. Wash and clean potatoes as above. Puncture (stab) each potato with a fork several times (this prevents them from exploding). Arrange on microwave dish in a fan-shaped arrangement, with ends of potatoes pointing toward center of dish. Cover loosely with sheet of waxed paper. Microwave for about six minutes. Turn potatoes upside down, rotate microwave dish 90 degrees, replace the waxed paper, and microwave for about another four minutes. If still not done, rotate dish again, and microwave for about two minutes. Remember: microwave ovens vary in strength and capacity, and in cooking times. Experiment to find the best cooking times for your microwave.

Heads up: no metal objects or objects with metal decoration in microwaves.

Meat loaf # 1

There are many meat loaf recipes, but very few bad ones. Here's a good all-purpose recipe.

one medium onion, chopped;
one rib celery, chopped;
one can condensed "cream of" soup; (such as cream of chicken, cream of broccoli, cream of mushroom, etc. Using any single soup will give a slightly different accent to the meat loaf. The soup provides a "binder" effect to hold all the ingredients together and makes the meat loaf moist).
one pound ground beef;
some fresh parsley, chopped, to taste;
one cup bread crumbs
ground pepper, to taste (if you're using regular condensed soup, you will not need to add salt);

Preheat oven to 350° F. Assemble ingredients. Mix all ingredients well, place in 9" x 5" x 4" loaf pan, and bake for about one hour. Serves four, with some leftovers.

Idea for leftovers:cold meat loaf tastes great in sandwiches. Add mustard and lettuce and perhaps a tomato slice for a really great lunch.

Green beans.

frozen green beans, one 16 ounce bag; or one ten ounce box

Open the bag of frozen green beans and shake out enough for four portions, or use entire box of frozen green beans. Place about 1/4 cup water in a saucepan, and cook, covered, over medium heat for about seven or eight minutes, or until beans are cooked to your liking. Some folks prefer their vegetables cooked crunchy and "bright." Others prefer them cooked longer, for a softer texture. Since the beans require the least cooking of the items in this menu, they should be prepared just before you plan to serve the meal. One half bag or one entire box each serves four.

Microwave variation for cooking vegetables: place beans, still frozen, in covered dish with just a little water, maybe a tablespoon. Cook for three minutes. Rotate microwave dish. Cook for another three minutes. Check for doneness, and stir. If necessary, cook for about one more minute. Again, microwaves vary, and you'll need to experiment to find optimum cooking times and procedures.

Heads up: when cooking foods in microwave, loosely cover them with waxed paper; or use covered microwave dish.

Why? Because some foods have this propensity to explode in a microwave. After you do "the salmon scrape" off the four walls, top and floor of the microwave a couple of times, you'll understand this more vividly. If you're using a tight covering, such as plastic wrap, always leave a corner open for steam to escape. Be careful when removing foods from the microwave--the dishes or containers can be very hot.

Bread and butter.

While the rest of the meal is cooking, set the table, and put the bread and butter out. Cover the bread with a cloth napkin to keep it fresh.

Iced tea.

You can brew fresh tea and pour it over tall glasses full of ice cubes. Or you can open the jar of instant iced tea, and using one spoonful per glass, mix it in a pitcher and serve it over ice. Add lemon if desired, ditto sugar. You decide. Powdered iced tea is a real time saver, and freshly brewed iced tea has a superior taste.

Ice cream

Buy a variety you enjoy.

Tuesday, Week One

Breakfast

Baked apples, toast, juice, coffee or tea.

Baked apples.

Friends who don't cook, when served this dish, will probably think you're simply amazing. Only you will know it's actually amazingly simple.

four apples, washed and cored (don't bother peeling them)
two Tbs. sugar
cinnamon, to taste
water

Preheat oven to 350° F. Place the apples in a baking dish, and pour water in dish to reach half way up the apples. Place about 1/4 of the sugar in the core of each apple. Sprinkle the apples with cinnamon; bake for about one hour, or until they reach the degree of doneness that you like. This recipe can be made the night before and heated in the morning; will keep several days in the refrigerator. Serves four.

Low fat and low salt info: apples are naturally low in salt and low in fat. This recipe contains no added salt or fat.

Variation: substitute maple syrup or honey for the sugar.

Idea for leftovers: Baked apples and vanilla ice cream make a great dessert. Baked apples are also good by themselves, as a snack item.

Lunch

Tuna salad (or sandwiches), fresh pear, beverage, rolls (if not serving sandwiches. Dessert: sliced peaches, canned or frozen.

Tuna salad #1.

Hey, hey, another classic American recipe. Here's what you need:

1 medium onion, cut up, enough to make about 1/4 cup of chopped onion
1 can tuna fish, drained
1 rib celery (one piece of the stalk, or bunch), chopped
1 teaspoon lemon juice
fresh parsley, if you have it around, chopped, perhaps 1/8 cup
2 Tbs mayonnaise, or to taste

Blend all ingredients well, refrigerate for 30 minutes or so, or, if you're in a hurry, serve at room temperature. Can be garnished with pickle chips or slices, radishes, celery, or carrots. Or even olives. Serves four.

Adaptation: for a tuna salad sandwich, add lettuce leaves and serve between two slices of bread.

Snack

Brownie or "blondie" (store bought or one you baked) and beverage. If you're baking the brownies, use a brownie mix; there are many good brands on the market. "Blondies" are brownies without chocolate, sometimes with a butterscotch flavor.

Tip: Read the package directions in the store and make certain you have all the ingredients needed, so that you can pick up any you don't have while you're shopping.

Tip: Brownies and other soft cookies can be stored in a tightly covered container. If you're not planning on eating them within a few days, they can be frozen.

"Scratch" brownies

In the event you don't have brownie mix around, and you don't want to purchase them, here is a good brownie recipe.

2 cups granulated sugar
1 cup (2 sticks) butter or margarine, melted
4 eggs, beaten
2 tsp. vanilla
1/4 c. cocoa
1 tsp. salt (optional)
1 and 1/2 cups flour, sifted
1/2 cup chopped nuts (optional)

Preheat oven to 375° F. Melt butter, beat eggs, mix together with other ingredients and pour into a 9 inch x 13 inch pan. Bake at 375° for 25 minutes or until knife blade or toothpick inserted into center comes out clean. Cool, cut into squares and serve. Makes 24 brownies.

Dinner

Ham steaks, peas, au gratin potatoes, green salad, beer bread, fresh strawberries, sparkling water.

Tip: Start the potatoes first. Next do the beer bread, then the ham steaks. While they are cooking, wash and hull the strawberries.

Au gratin potatoes.

2 large or 3 medium potatoes
1 cup milk
1/2 stick butter
2 ounces shredded cheese
sprinkling of Parmesan cheese
pepper
1/2 onion, sliced and separated into rings

Preheat oven to 375° F. Wash and thinly slice potatoes and onion. Layer bottom of ceramic baking dish with potato slices; add onion slices, and repeat until potatoes and onions have been used up. Pour milk over top of potatoes and onions. Cut butter into small pieces and place on top of potatoes. Sprinkle cheese over all. Salt and pepper to taste. Bake for about 45 minutes, then turn broiler on until cheese has browned. Serves four.

Tip: potatoes taste just great with the skin on, as long as you wash them first. Some recipes (such as many mashed potato recipes) do call for peeled potatoes. But most don't. An added benefit is that potato skin has a lot of fiber.

Ham steaks

Two medium sized ham steaks (about 8 ounces each)

Most ham steaks available today are actually thick slices of ham that have been precooked. Place in frying pan with a small amount of fat and saute until done. Or place in a preheated 350° F. oven for about 15 minutes. Some folks like to serve these with pineapple rings; or a molasses glaze, or both. Serves four.

Molasses glaze

2 TBS molasses
1 TBS butter

Heat molasses and butter together until butter melts, pour over ham steaks.

Green salad #1

Lettuce, Romaine or iceberg, about one large leaf per person to be served, plus one extra leaf, washed and torn into small pieces.
1 orange, sliced; slices cut into semi circles, orange peel, white lining beneath the skin, and seeds removed.
bottled French dressing

Wash lettuce, dry in colander or salad spinner or pat dry; mix with orange slices, toss with dressing. Canned mandarin orange sections can be substituted for fresh orange slices. Serves four.

Brad's beer bread

This is fun. And way easy to do. You need a cast iron frying pan or a 9 inch by 9 inch metal baking pan. The yeasts in the beer and the sodium in the baking mix help this bread rise. The alcohol in the beer evaporates in the baking process.

3 cups baking mix (also known as biscuit mix)
1 twelve ounce can beer, at room temperature
1 teaspoon granulated sugar (optional)
butter or shortening for greasing pan

Preheat oven to 375° F. Grease frying pan with butter or shortening. Pour in biscuit mix; then add beer and gently blend until well mixed. Place in hot oven for one hour. Bread is done when knife blade inserted into middle comes out clean. Store leftover bread in refrigerator (it will keep for a day or two).

Wednesday, Week One

Breakfast

Scrambled eggs, bacon, potatoes, coffee or tea, toast, jelly, orange juice.

Tip: Use some of the leftover beer bread from last night. Slice, split and toast in the oven under the broiler; or on the tray in your toaster oven. (The beer bread will crumble in a regular toaster.)

Egg Basics

Eggs are a really versatile and tasty food. They can be an ingredient in a dish, a component of a dish, a garnish, or a finished dish in their own right. It's a good idea to always have a few hard boiled eggs on hand for salads, snacking, or garnishes.

Scrambled, boiled, poached, fried, sunny side up or over easy, eggs are one of the best foods in the Gotta Cook Now!™ larder. Some of the things you can do with eggs include:

hard boiled eggs: use in egg salad; garnish green salad; use as part of composed salad; use for deviled eggs or stuffed eggs; place them in meat loaf (peel them first);

soft boiled eggs: eat as is; break over poached asparagus;

scrambled eggs: eat as is; stuff into ham rolls or tacos;

poached eggs: eat as is; eggs Benedict; serve on corned beef hash;

omelet: many variations, including western, ham, cheese, etc.

fried eggs eat as is; use in sandwiches.

About Cholesterol in Eggs

Yes, eggs have cholesterol. Yes, some people say the cholesterol in eggs isn't good for you. However, the amount of cholesterol in eggs is fairly moderate, and there are ways to minimize cholesterol from eggs while still enjoying egg products.

Suppose your doctor has told you to limit cholesterol intake (from eggs). Here are some things you can do:

a) throw away most of those yolks. If you're preparing scrambled eggs, and the recipe calls for four eggs, use six eggs and discard five of the yolks. This is about a 75% reduction in cholesterol; or

b) throw away *all* the yolks, using egg whites only; or

c) use a no-cholesterol egg substitute, sold in the dairy case or freezer section of your market.

Heads up: If you're under a doctor's care, be certain to consult your physician about your nutritional requirements

Tip: those non-cholesterol egg substitutes taste better if you add one or two ingredients to them such as green pepper, or chopped parsley.

Bacon

8 slices bacon

Place eight slices of bacon in a frying pan, and fry over medium heat, turning once, until done to the desired degree of crispness. Lift out with fork or metal spatula and place on dish, on which you have placed a paper towel. The paper towel absorbs fat from the bacon. Reserve the bacon fat. Serves four.

Microwave variation. Place bacon on sheet of paper towel on microwave-safe dish. Cover loosely with waxed paper. Cook for three minutes on medium. Rotate dish. Cook for another two minutes. Check and turn over. Cook two minutes more, or until the desired level of crispness is reached. (Experiment with times and power levels to obtain the best results with your microwave).

Tip: Use any leftovers for a bacon, lettuce and tomato sandwich (the fabled "BLT") later on.

Breakfast potatoes

two medium potatoes, sliced thin (leave skin on);
chopped onion, to taste
chopped parsley, to taste
bacon fat (salad oil or butter or margarine may be substituted)

Heat bacon fat over medium heat in same pan in which bacon was cooked. When hot, place potatoes in pan and brown, scraping potatoes off bottom of pan and turning occasionally, until done (about 15 minutes). Serves four.

While the potatoes are cooking you can set the table, make the coffee, pour the juice, and get a start on the toast. If you want to, you can put the cast iron frying pan into a 400 f. oven and cook the potatoes that way. Time is about 35 to 45 minutes.

Heads up: use potholders when taking items from a hot oven.

Tip: Some ovens are hotter than others. Ovens that are hotter are said to be "fast" and ovens that are cooler are said to be "slow." One way to determine whether your oven is cooking accurately is to use an oven thermometer. These are available at kitchen supply stores and many hardware stores. If your oven is hotter or slower than normal, make adjustments in your cooking times.

Scrambled eggs

The eggs can be scrambled in the same pan as the bacon was (if you like them cooked in bacon fat with little bits of bacon and potato in them) or in a separate pan cooked in butter or salad oil (if you don't).

4 eggs
1/8 cup (two ounces) milk
parsley garnish (optional).

Break the eggs into a 2 cup measuring cup and add the milk. Pierce the yolks, mix slightly, and pour into a frying pan in which you have warmed some cooking oil. Using a fork, spoon, or metal spatula, gently scramble the eggs, bringing the cooked portion from the bottom to the top, for a few minutes, until the desired degree of doneness is obtained. (Some folks like scrambled eggs dry and some folks like them runny. Pay your money; take your choice). Put the eggs on a platter. Garnish them with fresh parsley, if desired. Serves four

Garnish Basics

It's already late in this book, but not too late, to tell you about garnishes. Why all the fuss about garnishes, anyway? Well, it's been proven that garnishes enhance the "eye appeal" of foods. They add color or contrast and therefore, interest to the plate. Chopped fresh parsley, or dried parsley make an easy garnishes. So do pimento slices or red pepper rings or strips. Here are some good garnishes:

Fresh parsley, in sprigs or chopped: use in scrambled eggs, pasta dishes, potatoes, composed salads, deviled eggs, tomato slices, potatoes, soups, salads, rice, casseroles, and on chicken and fish.

Green olives: adds good contrast to sandwich plates and salads.

Pickles: use chips with hamburgers, gherkins with cold meats, dill spears with sandwiches or chopped in some cold salads

Orange slices: use on sandwich plates, breakfast platters, fish. An orange slice placed next to a parsley sprig adds lots of color to a bland dish.

Lemon slices: same uses as orange slices, plus chicken, seafood

Pimento: chopped pimento is great when you need a bit of red to brighten a plate. Usually sold chopped or whole, in jars.

Other garnishes appear throughout the book, where appropriate.

Idea for leftovers: use leftover bacon in spaghetti carbonara (recipe for spaghetti carbonara is provided as an alternate recipe in tonight's dinner menu).

Lunch

Franks and beans, sliced tomatoes with vinaigrette dressing, bread and butter, iced tea, apple.

Franks and beans

four frankfurters
one 15 ounce can baked beans
one small onion or 1/2 medium onion
2 Tbs. oil

Heat the oil in a medium skillet and saute the onions over medium heat until softened (about 5 minutes). Cut up the franks into one inch pieces and add to the onions, cooking about three minutes. Add the beans, and heat, stirring occasionally, until warmed through. Serve with bread and butter. This recipe may also be prepared in a covered, microwave-safe dish, in the microwave. Use medium power, for about six minutes; rotating dish 90 degrees midway through cooking. Serves four.

Sliced tomatoes with vinaigrette dressing

two medium tomatoes
vinaigrette dressing (recipe below)

Slice two medium tomatoes, place on individual dishes on lettuce leaf, if desired. Serve with vinaigrette dressing. Serves four.

Vinaigrette dressing

3 Tbs. olive oil
1 Tbs. vinegar
pinch salt
black pepper, to taste.

Mix ingredients well and drizzle over tomatoes..

Snack

Green pepper rings, crackers, cola drink.

Green pepper rings

1 green bell pepper

Wash pepper, and remove stem and core, along with seeds. Slice across the pepper to make rings. Serves one or two.

Dinner

American spaghetti, red sauce I, green salad II, Garlic bread I, red wine, coffee, and tira misu I.

Timing Tip: Make the tira misu first, then the sauce. While the sauce is simmering, put water on to boil for the pasta, and make the salad.

Pasta Sauce Basics

There are thousands of variations on sauce for pasta. Most familiar are various red sauces; there are white sauces, green sauces, vegetable sauces, and seafood sauces, as well. The sauce in this recipe is the classic "meat sauce" beloved of college dining halls and cheap restaurants. Only this version isn't cheap, and has lots of subtlety and nuance. A tip of the hat to my Aunt Kay (Caterina) who taught me to make this sauce.

Red sauce #I

1 garlic clove, peeled and crushed
1 medium onion, chopped
3 Tbs olive oil
1 28 ounce can tomatoes. whole or crushed, or whole or crushed in added puree.
1 pound ground chuck (or 1 pound ground turkey)
1 eight ounce can tomato sauce
pinch ground oregano, or to taste (less is better)
2 pinches ground basil, or to taste (more is better)
some fresh parsley, chopped, to taste
1 Tbs. red wine (optional)
1 tsp granulated sugar (optional)

Peel garlic clove and crush, using the flat side of a knife; place in skillet, and pour olive oil over the garlic. Turn on heat, and brown garlic in oil, then remove garlic and discard. Add chopped onions and saute until soft. Add ground meat and brown. Pour off fat, and scrape onion, meat, drippings, and any browned bits into a medium size pot. Add tomatoes, tomato sauce and seasonings.

Simmer 1/2 hour, stirring occasionally. At this time, correct the seasoning, add any additional seasoning, salt, pepper, etc., and perhaps some fresh parsley. Add 1 Tbs. red wine (from the wine you plan to serve with dinner) and 1 tsp. sugar. Why? These latter ingredients add "depth," "balance," and "complexity" to the sauce (and they don't add this stuff in the college dining hall). Simmer another 15 minutes. Viola! Spaghetti sauce (Red sauce #I). Serves four, with leftovers.

Time-saving alternative: use a canned or bottled spaghetti sauce.

If your schedule does not permit making the sauce from scratch, never fear--there are lots of good prepared spaghetti sauces on the market--buy a quart size jar of a flavor you like. Open the jar, heat the contents in a saucepan, then pour over cooked spaghetti or other type of pasta.

American spaghetti

1 pound spaghetti
1 tsp. olive oil
1 pinch salt
5 quarts water (some recipes call for 10 quarts water. Use different amounts until you find the quantity of water that is right for you).

While the sauce is cooking, put a pot of water, 5 to 10 quarts, on high heat, covered, and bring to a boil. Add a small amount of olive oil or other cooking oil. Why? It makes the pasta less sticky. When the water has come to a full rolling boil, add the spaghetti. You can use regular spaghetti, or thin spaghetti. Cook, uncovered, stirring occasionally, until spaghetti is cooked (should be slightly resistant to the tooth, or "al dente," although some people like it more thoroughly cooked. You decide). Two or three minutes before you drain the spaghetti, make ready a platter or large dish. Spoon about two Tbs of sauce on the bottom of the dish. Drain the spaghetti. Serves four.

Tip: There is no need to rinse spaghetti after it has been drained, if you plan to serve it immediately. If you wish to "hold" the spaghetti for more than a few minutes, do this: leave the spaghetti in a colander and plunge it into a bowl of cold water, until it has cooled (about two minutes). Drain again, then place back in the pot it was cooked in, which has been removed from the heat. Toss with olive oil to prevent sticking.

Alternate recipe for dinner, Wednesday, Week One

Spaghetti carbonara

This pasta sauce cooks in the hot pasta.

4 to six slices cooked bacon, crumbled
1 egg, lightly beaten,
1 Tbs. butter (1/8 of a stick of butter) cut into small pieces
small amount milk (about 1 Tbs.)
Parmesan cheese
black pepper

Crumble the bacon and set aside. Lightly beat the egg and mix with the butter and the milk. The butter will still be in individual pieces. Drain the pasta, and return to pasta pot. Remove pasta pot from direct heat. Toss the egg, milk and butter mixture into the hot pasta, followed immediately by the bacon. The egg mixture will cook in the hot pasta and the butter will melt. Serve immediately, topped with Parmesan cheese and the black pepper. Serves four.

Ideas for leftovers--

If you have leftover spaghetti or other pasta that has been sauced, it is terrific reheated and served for lunch;

If you have leftover unsauced pasta, try it with a butter sauce (melt half a stick of butter and mix with some chopped fresh parsley); or with a white clam sauce (sold by the can in the ethnic foods section of your supermarket);

If you have any leftover sauce, it might be particularly good served with stuffed green peppers and green peas;

What if you don't have time to prepare a complex pasta sauce? Use one of the prepared sauces that are sold in most stores, or make:

Another alternative sauce for this meal.

Quick Pasta Sauce

1 28 ounce can of tomatoes, either whole, chopped or crushed
1 6 ounce can of tomato paste
1 Tbs. dried basil (or 3 Tbs fresh basil, chopped)
salt and pepper to taste
garlic powder (optional)

Place tomatoes and paste in pan and bring just to a boil. Add basil and garlic powder, if you are using it, salt and pepper, and cook just below boiling for five minutes. Serves four, with leftovers. This recipe makes a terrific quick sauce. Serves four.

Salad Basics

Generally, salads are made up of washed, uncooked vegetables, principally leafy ones, usually tossed and coated with a flavored dressing.

Tossed green salad # II

Lettuce leaves, Romaine or iceberg, or both, about four of each or eight leaves total, washed and torn into small pieces.
A few onion slices, sliced thinly and divided into rings, perhaps one or two slices worth
Lemon dressing (recipe below)
Fresh parsley.

Wash the lettuce, removing any brown spots, and pat dry with paper towels or use a salad spinner if you have one. Tear the lettuce (cutting with scissors or knife makes edges turn brown) into small pieces. Add the onion rings and parsley. Just before serving, toss with the lemon dressing. Serves four.

Lemon dressing

juice of one-half lemon, or about 2 TBS
olive oil or salad oil, about six TBS
pinch salt (optional)
black pepper
garlic (optional)

Use about a 3 to 1 oil to lemon juice ratio. In this recipe, lemon juice is substituted for the vinegar. Six Tbs. oil and two Tbs. lemon juice should do it. Add some salt or pepper. If you aren't a big garlic fan, but want a mild garlic flavor, peel a garlic clove and rub the salad bowl with it, then discard. If you want a stronger garlic flavor, mix the dressing the night before, and place a peeled, crushed garlic clove in the dressing. Remove garlic clove before serving salad.

Salad dressings tend to separate, so stir well or shake just before tossing into salad. Of course, if you're going to shake the dressing, use a sealed container.

Alternative: if you're short of time, use a bottled salad dressing.

Variations: to make a dressing reminiscent of the Provencal region of France, add some prepared Dijon mustard, perhaps 2 tsps, or 1 tsp. of dry mustard.

To make a dressing that is more Italian, add some chopped oregano and a bit of minced garlic; or substitute red wine vinegar if you have some.

Tip: it is said, "one should be a spendthrift with the oil and a pauper with the vinegar."

Salads can also contain no leafy vegetables; can be hot; and, instead of being tossed, can be designed and elaborately planned. The latter type of salad is known as *salade composee*. You've already made an elemental cold *salade composee* when you sliced those tomatoes in today's lunch menu. It was easy, right?

Tira mi su # I

12 to 16 ladyfingers (found at bakeries, or in the baked goods section of your supermarket).
1/2 pint whipping cream (or use frozen whipped topping)
strong leftover coffee, about one cup
rum or coffee liqueur, or creme de cacao, about 1 ounce
cinnamon and cocoa, about 1 tsp. (that's teaspoon) of each.

Use a glass 8"x 8" x 2" baking dish. Split ladyfingers lengthwise. Dip some of the ladyfingers *very fast* into the coffee. Layer them on bottom of baking dish. Sprinkle some of the liqueur on the ladyfingers. Sprinkle a small amount of the cinnamon on the ladyfingers. Cover with whipped cream. Repeat with the rest of the ladyfingers and place on top of first layer. Repeat the whipped cream. Dust with the cinnamon and cocoa. Refrigerate for about one hour. (So, prepare this before dinner.) Serves four.

Whipped Cream

1/2 pint whipping cream
1/2 tsp. vanilla extract

Place the cream in a chilled bowl. Using chilled beaters or a chilled whisk, beat until soft peaks are formed when you lift the beaters.

Thursday, Week One

Breakfast

Waffles, syrup, butter, strawberries, juice, coffee or tea.

Waffles

Use frozen waffles, prepare according to package directions, and serve with butter or margarine and syrup.

Fresh Strawberries

Wash and hull (remove the green tops) the strawberries, cut up if desired, sprinkle with about 1 tsp sugar, and serve.

Lunch

Peanut butter and banana sandwich, carrot sticks, beverage (maybe iced tea), apple for dessert.

Peanut butter and banana sandwich

bread, 2 slices per person
bananas, about one per sandwich
peanut butter, about 1 TBS per sandwich, or more or less to taste

Take two slices of bread and spread each thinly with peanut butter. Slice a banana and arrange on one of the bread slices. Top with the other bread slice, cut in half, and serve.

Variation: try bacon, onion or apple, instead of banana.

Snack

Cookies and beverage, maybe milk or juice

Easy lemon crisp cookies

1 stick (1 half cup) room temperature butter or margarine
1/3 cup sugar, granulated
1 egg
1/4 tsp salt (optional)
1/2 to 1 tsp vanilla extract (buy the real thing, not the imitation)
1/4 teaspoon grated lemon rind
1 cup all purpose flour, sifted (use a wire mesh colander if you have no flour sifter)

Preheat oven to 375° F. While the oven is heating, assemble the ingredients. Cream butter and sugar together using a fork to mash the sugar into the butter. Add the egg, lightly beaten, salt, vanilla, and lemon rind. and mix. Add flour and mix all ingredients well, to form a dough. Form one-inch balls with the dough, and flatten by hand, on a cookie tray, leaving space between these little cookie balls, as they will expand during baking. Bake for about 12 minutes, or until the edges turn a crisp light brown, whichever comes first. Remove from oven, cool. Store in a covered cookie jar. Makes 24 to 30 cookies.

Idea for leftovers--serve leftover cookies with ice cream.

Dinner

Pork chop and rice casserole, bread and butter, coffee, vanilla ice cream.

Tip: pork and pork products, such as bacon, should always be cooked well done.

Pork chop and rice casserole

Viola! The rice cooks in the tomato juice, the pork chops absorb the flavor of the vegetables and you have a smashing one dish supper that will have them clamoring for seconds. Or at least saying, "hey, this isn't bad."

four pork chops
1 cup rice, white, brown, or blend of each
1 green pepper, washed, cored, seeded, and cut up
1 medium onion, peeled, and cut up
1 or 2 ribs celery, washed, trimmed and cut up
1 46 ounce can tomato juice
black pepper to taste
salt (optional)

Preheat oven to 450° F. Place dry uncooked rice in bottom of covered casserole dish and mix with cut up vegetables. Place pork chops on top of rice and vegetables. Pour the 46 ounce can of tomato juice over the pork chops and vegetables and cover the casserole dish. Place in oven for one hour. Serves four.

While the casserole is cooking, set the table, get the bread and butter ready, and relax for a while, checking the casserole occasionally. If you're really feeling industrious, throw a green salad together to serve with the casserole.

Idea for leftovers--serve for lunch with a tossed green salad or a sliced orange salad.

Friday, Week One

Breakfast

Cold cereal with strawberries or bananas, toast and butter, fruit juice, coffee, tea or milk.

Variation: substitute blueberries or canned peaches or pears for the strawberries.

Lunch

Hamburgers on hamburger buns, ketchup, mustard, relish, onions, home fries, green beans. Cola drink, ice cream with some of the leftover cookies.

Hamburger Basics

When a high school buddy heard about this book, he said, "You really know menus for forty different days?" Well, yes. So do you. Take hamburger, for instance. Hamburger meat is beef that has been chopped, with a bit of fat added to it. The more costly the cut used for the hamburger, the less fat it contains. Ground beef is extremely versatile and can be used in lots of recipes.

With a pound of hamburger meat, you can make:

burgers
spaghetti sauce with meat (loose hamburger)
spaghetti sauce with meat balls
Swedish meatballs
chili
sloppy Joes
Salisbury steak
meat loaf #I
meat loaf #II
hamburger Stroganov

--and that's just the beginning.

Pan fried hamburgers

1 pound hamburger (ground chuck is recommended, but you can use other varieties)
half of one medium onion, chopped
half of one medium onion, sliced
cooking oil, small amount
four slices cheese
condiments--mustard, relish, ketchup, pickles, onion slices, whatever you like
4 hamburger buns
salt (optional)
pepper

Peel the onion. Divide into two halves. Chop half of it into fairly small pieces, less than 1/4 inch x 1/4 inch. Put the oil into the frying pan, and turn heat on low. Mix the onion with the hamburger meat and divide into four burger-sized patties. Add salt and pepper to taste and place in frying pan, where the oil has been heated. Cook to the desired state of doneness, turning once. (To test, cut one burger open with knife). Slice the second half of the onion and divide into rings to place on top of hamburgers. Serves four.

Variation: can be made without the onion, if you wish.

Timing tip: Cook the potatoes first, then the hamburgers.

Home fried potatoes

four medium potatoes, washed and sliced. (Use canned if you wish to save time. Rinse and drain the canned potatoes.)
1/2 onion

Cook the potatoes first and keep warm in the oven while the burgers are cooking. Slice the half onion into rings and saute over medium heat until soft. Add the potatoes, cooking until nicely browned. If you have a second frying pan, fry the hamburgers in the other pan while the potatoes are cooking.

Idea for leftovers--home fries can be reheated and served for breakfast with eggs.

Snack

Popcorn, small can of juice

Dinner

Tuna noodle casserole, broccoli, applesauce, drop biscuits. Coffee, cookies, fresh strawberries.

Tuna noodle casserole

This recipe is very "forgiving" and can be varied considerably.

1 medium onion, chopped
1 can tuna fish, drained
1 rib celery, sliced crosswise into 1/2 inch pieces.
1 can condensed cream of mushroom, celery, or asparagus soup
1/2 soup can milk
1 tsp sherry (optional)
1/2 pound elbow macaroni, cooked
fresh parsley, cut up, and divided. "Divided" is a cooking term indicating use of some of the ingredient one way in the recipe, and the rest of it, *some other* way. In this case, put half the parsley into the casserole. Garnish each serving with the rest.
black pepper.

Preheat the oven to 350° F. Bring water to boil for the elbow macaroni. Meanwhile, wash and slice the celery and chop the parsley. Open the soup and mix with the milk, and, if you wish, the sherry. Cook the elbow macaroni, stirring occasionally. Open and flake the tuna fish, and drain macaroni. In a covered baking dish, mix tuna, celery, 1/2 of the parsley, onion, and some black pepper. Cover and bake for about one hour. Garnish with the remainder of the parsley. Serves four, six in a pinch.

Drop biscuits

two cups baking mix
2/3 cup milk

Preheat the oven to 450° F. Pour the milk into the baking mix with and blend, (this will make a soft dough) and drop onto cookie sheet. Bake in oven for about 15 minutes or until done to the brownness you like. Serve with butter. Makes ten to twelve biscuits. This recipe is so easy, you'll find yourself making biscuits very often. This recipe can be cut in half.

Alternative: store-bought biscuits that you bake yourself. These taste pretty good, and there are a lot of varieties. Experiment with them until you find the varieties you like best.

Store bought biscuits

Buy one of those tubes of biscuit dough sold in your grocer's dairy case and follow directions on the tube. Remember: some store-bought things taste better than what you can prepare at home. Some taste about the same. In the case of biscuits, homemade biscuits may taste better than those from the store-bought tube. You may be in a really big hurry, or you may prefer store-bought biscuits. You decide.

Broccoli

1 head broccoli
butter, about 1 Tbs. (optional)
lemon wedges

Wash and cut the broccoli into individual stalks. Cook in boiling water, and when the broccoli turns bright green, remove it from the heat. Plunge into a pot or large bowl of very cold water. This stops the cooking process. Just before serving, melt a little butter in a saucepan, and gently warm the broccoli in the butter. Serve with lemon wedges. Serves four.

Quicker broccoli

1 ten ounce box frozen broccoli, or as much as you want from a 16 ounce bag of frozen broccoli cuts
lemon wedges

Put the broccoli in a saucepan with a small amount of water. Cook until heated through. Serve with lemon wedges. Faster, considerably less trouble, and not that bad. Serves four or so.

Idea for leftovers--chop the broccoli and serve cold with an oil and vinegar dressing and tomato slices as a side salad..

Saturday, Week One

Breakfast

Pancakes, syrup, butter; orange slices; bacon; coffee or tea.

Pancakes

2 cups biscuit mix (baking mix)
1 and 1/4 cups milk

Grease griddle or cast iron frying pan and place over medium heat (you can use margarine, butter, or oil). Mix milk into baking mix, and pour onto hot griddle, on large spoonful for each pancake. Cook on one side until bubbles appear on the uncooked surface; turn over, using pancake turner and cook on other side until done. Serve with syrup and butter. Serves four.

Tip: leftover pancakes can be stored in the refrigerator.

Variation: substitute breakfast sausage or ham for the bacon.

Uptown pancakes

Same recipe as above, but add one slightly beaten egg to batter and mix well. Pancakes will be lighter, richer, fluffier.

Variations: Instead of bottled pancake syrup, try maple syrup; molasses; a simple syrup made of 1 cup sugar, 1 cup water and some cinnamon; powdered sugar; jelly or jam; corn syrup; or granulated sugar mixed with cinnamon.

Lunch

Egg salad sandwich, cucumber slices, chicken boullion, milk.

Chicken boullion

1 chicken boullion cube per serving
Eight ounces water per serving
Parsley leaves (optional)

Place eight ounces of water in a saucepan. Add one boullion cube, heat to boiling, and remove from heat when dissolved. Garnish with parsley. Serve with crackers. Serves one. Add one cube and eight ounces of water per additional person.to be served.

Low salt option. Chicken boullion can be purchased in cans, already prepared, with a lower salt content. Just open the can and heat.

Egg salad sandwich

For each sandwich, use:

two slices bread
two hard cooked eggs, peeled and chopped
1 rib celery, chopped
1 tablespoon mayonnaise
1 teaspoon mustard
pinch fresh parsley
chopped onion to taste (optional)
salt and pepper to taste

Mix dry ingredients together, add mustard, mayonnaise and mix; place between two slices of bread; cut in halves and serve. Serves one; this recipe can be doubled, tripled, or quadrupled easily.

Snack

Have an apple, or substitute a pear, plum, or nectarine. A wedge of the cheddar cheese you bought. A cup of tea.

Appetizer

Chips with onion dip.

Onion dip

eight ounces (1 cup) sour cream
1 envelope dry onion soup mix

Place sour cream in bowl and add onion soup mix. Blend. Serve with chips or crackers.

Garnish ideas: garnish with red pepper ring or with sliced olives. or sprinkle chopped fresh parsley on the surface.

Variations: add some finely chopped celery; or some chopped fresh parsley; or a dash or two of hot sauce or hot pepper flakes.

Low fat variation. Use non-fat sour cream or a mixture of nonfat sour cream and plain nonfat yogurt.

Dinner

Steaks, baked potatoes, corn, bread and butter, salad. Red wine. Lemon crisp cookies with ice cream.

About steaks

Buy one steak per person. Size can range from about four ounces each to perhaps eight ounces each, for hearty eaters.

Grilled steaks

If you have a barbecue (gas or charcoal) grill, light the gas or follow the directions on the bag of charcoal, light the coals, wait until they turn white, and grill the steaks until the desired degree of doneness.

Heads up: This seldom takes more than ten or twelve minutes, so don't leave the grill while the steaks are cooking. Only use a charcoal grill outdoors.

Tip: Use long-handled tools and well-insulated potholders while working with grills.

Oven-broiled steaks

No charcoal grill? No problem. Place steaks on oven broiler tray and place under broiler, turning when they reach the desired degree of doneness. Most ovens broil at about 500 degrees f. To broil in most ovens, the oven door is left open about an inch or so.

Pan fried steaks

We once had this roommate who worked as cook for a frat house. He flat out fried just about *everything*. This is how he fried steaks:

Rub a frying pan with garlic clove, and discard garlic. Put olive oil or other cooking oil in pan, and heat over medium flame or burner; place steaks in pan and fry, until bottom is brown and middle is the way you like it; turn and repeat process until steaks are done.

Idea for leftovers--slice leftover steak thinly and use in sandwiches..

Baked potatoes

See baked potato recipe in dinner, Monday, Week One (page 64).

Variation: buy a box or bag of frozen French fries and prepare according to package directions.

Corn

Open a bag of frozen corn and pour some out, and heat the corn according to package directions until done. Or use canned corn, and warm in a saucepan. Feeling adventurous? You can make:

Western corn

Chop about 1/4 onion and saute about five minutes, until soft. Add 1/4 cup chopped green pepper, and saute another two or three minutes. Place in saucepan and add corn, (drain first if using canned corn). Heat until done and season to taste. Four servings.

Sunday, Week One

Breakfast

Waffles with syrup, or with sauteed apples and bananas, juice, coffee, tea, or milk.

Waffles

Use frozen waffles. Follow directions on package.

Sauteed apples and bananas

2 apples, sliced (peel them if you want to; you don't need to)
1 banana, peeled and sliced
butter for sauteing
molasses, about 1/4 cup

In frying pan, melt butter over medium heat; add apples, stir gently to coat with butter and saute for two or three minutes; add bananas, and saute about one minute. Drizzle molasses over apples and bananas, stirring gently. Serve over waffles.

Lunch

Salmon rice salad, sliced tomatoes, rye bread, cola drink.

Boiled rice (for salmon rice salad)

1/2 cup rice
1 Tbs olive oil
1 cup water, plus 2 Tbs water

In a saucepan mix the uncooked rice and the olive oil. Add 1 full cup, plus a bit more, water to the saucepan. Cover, and bring to the boil. When the rice has come to a full, rolling boil lower the heat to "low" and cook until the rice is ready (water will be absorbed). White rice takes about 20 minutes; brown rice about 45 minutes. Or use one of the brands of "quick" rice; they take about five minutes to cook after the water and rice has begun to boil.

Salmon rice salad

1 cup cooked rice (see preceding recipe)
1 fifteen ounce can salmon, red or pink (or poach the fresh salmon you bought and chop it up; or use leftover salmon that you have prepared previously)
1 medium green pepper, washed, cored, and chopped
1 rib celery, chopped
3 green onions, chopped, or 1/4 medium onion, chopped
fresh parsley, chopped to make about 1/4 cup
mayonnaise, about 2 Tbs.
lemon juice, optional
dash or two of black pepper

While the rice is cooking, open the salmon, and use a fork to break it into flakes. Pick out the larger bones, if you wish. Chop vegetables, mix with salmon. Add mayonnaise, sprinkle with lemon juice and black pepper. May be served at room temperature, or you can refrigerate it for an hour or two and serve it cold. If you refrigerate it, re-toss before serving.

Variations: this recipe can also be made using tuna fish, canned halibut or mackerel. Or you could substitute one cup of cooked chicken, which has been chopped into bite sized pieces, for the fish..

Snack

Pretzel sticks (bought at store) and an orange.

Low fat variation: Use fat free pretzel products.

Dinner

Chicken artichoke bake, oven roasted potatoes, green salad #1 with blue cheese, white wine spritzers, sandy tarts, coffee or tea.

About Chicken

Chicken is a very adaptable and relatively inexpensive food. A friend who has been cooking for forty-odd years, said recently that "a chicken is a chicken is a chicken. . .*however: tomato sauce* makes it Italian; *white wine* makes it French; *pineapple and brown sugar* make it Hawaiian; *green pepper and soy sauce* make it Oriental; *curry, yogurt and raisins* make it Indian; *paprika and sour cream* makes it Hungarian."

Chicken artichoke bake

1 medium chicken cut up.
1 medium onion, sliced
2 or 3 medium potatoes
1 6.5 ounce jar marinated artichokes (reserve marinade)
1 carrot
parsley, to taste
salt and pepper, to taste
1 chicken bullion cube

Preheat oven to 375° F. Rinse chicken pieces, pat dry with paper towels, and place in open roasting pan. Peel onion and cut into wedges. Wash potatoes and carrots and cut into 1 inch pieces. Place 2 Tbs. of olive oil and marinade from the artichokes in a bowl. Coat vegetables and onions with the oil and the marinade. Place in baking pan with the chicken. Bake 90 minutes to 1 hour 45 minutes, turning and basting once or twice. Serves four.

Green salad # II with blue cheese

Prepare green salad #II as you did on Wednesday (page 71); crumble blue cheese on top. Serve with vinaigrette dressing.

Easy wine spritzers

Into four wine glasses gently pour some club soda or sparkling water over ice cubes. Add white wine of your choice. Garnish with lemon wedges. Four servings.

Non-alcoholic alternative: use cranberry juice cocktail instead of wine and add sparkling water.

24 ounces cranberry juice cocktail
1 liter or 1 quart sparkling water or club soda

Place ice cubes in four glasses. Pour cranberry juice cocktail into glasses over ice cubes until glasses are about half full . Gently pour sparkling water into glasses. Serves four.

Sandy tarts

1/2 pound butter (two sticks)
2 cups granulated sugar
3 eggs, (separate one yolk from one white and reserve white)
2 tsps. vanilla extract
4 cups all purpose flour, sifted
1/8 tsps. salt (optional)
cinnamon and granulated sugar, for topping

Preheat oven to 350° F. Cream butter and sugar together. Beat in eggs one at a time, adding lone yolk last. Add vanilla. Add flour and mix well. Roll fairly thin. Cut into small rectangles. Brush the surface of each rectangle with the remaining egg white. Sprinkle with cinnamon and granulated sugar mixture. Bake about eight minutes. Makes about six dozen.

Idea for leftovers--serve with chocolate or butterscotch pudding as a snack.

Chocolate pudding

One 4 and 1/2 ounce box chocolate pudding mix
2 cups milk (skim milk can be used)

Place pudding mix in saucepan, and add milk. Stir continuously over medium heat, until pudding thickens. Place in small dessert dishes and chill in refrigerator. Makes four 1/2 cup servings.

Convenience alternative: buy pudding ready made, in individual cans.

Chapter Four

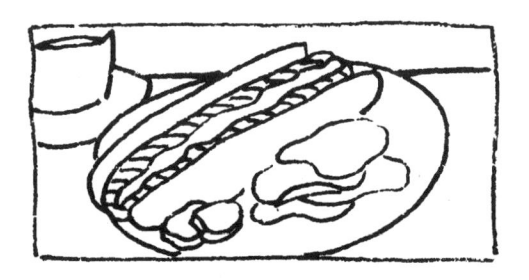

Stocking Up: Week Two

CONGRATULATIONS! Week One, with its challenges and glowing successes, is behind you. What are you going to do differently in Week Two? You are going to cook with more flair. Your presentations are going to be more scintillating. And you will be stocking a wider variety of goods from the store.

Remember, last week you bought just four or five spices and herbs: parsley, garlic, oregano, basil and cinnamon, plus salt and pepper. You should have plenty of those items left. This week, pick up some additional items, such as nutmeg, sage, dill weed, cloves and ground red pepper (see About Herbs and Spices, pages 52-56)

Dairy products

Inventory what's left from last week and replace the items you have used. In addition, buy:

sour cream: one eight ounce container of sour cream.

yogurt: one eight ounce container of plain yogurt.

Tip: If yogurt is something you already use as a food, of course buy more of it than a single container. If you haven't eaten yogurt before, you may enjoy it. Yogurt is a pretty nutritious item, and comes in a lot of flavors. Experiment to see which you like; yogurt is pretty good served with dry cereal, or with fruit. Yogurt makes a great sauce, alone or mixed with other ingredients. There are nonfat and lowfat yogurts on the market. Lots of people eat fresh yogurt, often with fruit, as dessert. And thousands more have made frozen yogurt a viable alternative to ice cream.

cheese: buy some different kinds than last week. For example:

cheddar cheese, eight ounces, whole or shredded.

cottage cheese, eight ounces, and ricotta, eight ounces; or, if ricotta is not available, pick up one pound of cottage cheese.

8 ounces cream cheese, if you will be making the carrot cake

mozzarella cheese, eight ounces, shredded.

Parmesan cheese (if not bought last week), four to eight ounces.

Meat and Fish

Beef: one 2 -1/2 pound chuck roast

Hamburger: about 2 pounds ground beef (or ground beef, pork and veal mixture, for meat loaf)

Chicken: one whole chicken 3 to 3-1/2 pounds

Pork: one small roast, boneless, about 2.5 to 3.5 pounds.

Produce

cantaloupe: one medium cantaloupe

carrots: if none in inventory, buy one bunch carrots, or one pound prewashed baby carrots (three pounds if making the carrot cake) cucumbers: two medium sized cucumbers.

eggplant: one medium purple eggplant

grapefruit: two grapefruit (to serve four, increase if more people)

grapes: one good sized bunch green or red seedless grapes

lettuce: how's the lettuce supply? If you need some, buy a head of the kind you didn't buy last week, such as Boston or bibb.

endive: one small head. This is a good leafy vegetable for salads.

scallions: one bunch. These are the tall, green onions with white roots.

tomatoes: four or five medium tomatoes

zucchini: two or three firm green zucchini squash

Frozen (or Fresh) Products

squash: a box of frozen bright orange squash

sorbet: get some sorbet, or if your store has it, some Italian ice.

pound cake: about 10 to 16 ounce size, fresh or frozen.

Staples

lunch meat: one twelve ounce can lunch meat, such as Spam®.

Canned Foods

marinated artichoke hearts: six ounces.

beets: one can, sliced, if you didn't get them last week.

caviar: Buy one 2 ounce jar of lumpfish caviar (black or red).

corned beef hash: 1 fifteen-ounce or 16-ounce can.

potatoes: one 16 ounce can, sliced or whole, canned.

deviled ham: 1 can.

salad or cocktail shrimp: 1 four ounce can or jar.

Dried Foods

baking soda: 1 eight ounce box, if you will be making carrot cake.

baking powder: 1 small can, if you will be making carrot cake.

ground nutmeg, 1 small jar or can

chopped leaf sage, 1 small jar or can

curry powder, small jar

dill weed, 1 small jar

cloves, 1 small jar, ground.

raisins: 1 small box dried raisins, if making carrot cake.

red pepper (hot pepper), ground, 1 small jar

Baked Goods

bread: Buy some if needed. Remember, bread freezes well and defrosts quickly. Get some bread sticks, too.

Cake, 1 frozen carrot cake, about 10 ounces; 1 frozen pound cake; or you may be ready for a different variety. If so, try devil's food instead of carrot.

Tip: If you are planning to make your carrot cake from scratch, be certain you have all of those ingredients.

English muffins. Four muffins for one evening meal (to serve four).

Chapter Five

Menus and Recipes for Week Two

ALL RIGHT, what's on tap for Week Two? First, congratulate yourself on your successes during the last week. Now it's time to develop your roasting, presentation, and baking skills.

Week Two Menus

Monday

Breakfast: Baked pears or apples, corn bread, butter, jelly; coffee, tea or other beverage, fruit juice.

Lunch: Yogurt, fresh fruit, bread sticks (or other bread of your choice), iced tea.

Snack: Peanuts, cola drink, seedless grapes

Dinner: English muffin pizzas, green salad #III with artichoke dressing, red wine, Italian ice or sorbet.

Tuesday

Breakfast: Scrambled eggs, potatoes and peppers, fruit juice, toast and butter, tea or coffee.

Lunch: Sliced ham and roasted pepper sandwich, with lettuce and mayonnaise; apple or pear; beverage.

Snack: Celery stuffed with cream cheese, mineral water.

Dinner: Poached fish, parsley potatoes, green beans, never bake cheesecake, coffee or tea.

Wednesday

Breakfast: Beer coffee cake, blueberries, orange juice, coffee or tea.

Lunch: Corned beef hash, poached eggs, tomato slices, toast, cola drinks

Snack: Cucumber rounds with cottage cheese or sour cream dollops, iced tea

Dinner: Whole roasted chicken, curried rice, green peppers and zucchini, bread and butter, white wine, sorbet.

Thursday

Breakfast: Cold cereal, sliced banana, toast, orange juice, coffee or tea.

Lunch: Hot dogs, sauerkraut, mustard, buns, baked beans, milk, ice cream.

Snack: Potato chips, cola beverage

Dinner: Three cheese macaroni, artichoke and Romaine salad, bread, butter, Ida's apple dessert, coffee or tea.

Friday

Breakfast: cantaloupe, cottage cheese, fruit juice, toast or muffin, coffee or tea.

Lunch: Leftovers! How about the leftover macaroni from Thursday night's dinner, mixed with some hot dogs that you have cut up and heated in a frying pan. Toss this with a dash or two of hot pepper and serve with celery sticks and bell pepper rings, bread, and soft drinks.

Snack: Apple or pear, bread sticks.

Dinner: Eggplant bake, green salad, hard rolls, orange slices with liqueur, coffee or tea.

Saturday

Breakfast: hot cereal, grapes, fruit juice, coffee or tea

Lunch: pasta with cottage cheese and spinach, tomato wedges, bread, red wine

Snack: banana and cookie or brownie

Dinner: Meat loaf #2, green peas, biscuits, rice pudding, coffee or tea.

Sunday

Breakfast: 1/2 grapefruit, oatmeal, toast, coffee or tea.

Lunch: Deviled ham, sharp cheddar, and green pepper sandwich on whole wheat bread

Snack: Coffee cookies, skim milk

Hors d'ouevre: Cucumber rounds with sour cream and caviar

Dinner: Oven pot roast with vegetables, endive and Romaine (or other lettuce) salad with Beth's dressing, carrot cake

Monday, Week Two

Breakfast

Baked apples or pears, corn bread, butter, jelly, fruit juice, coffee or tea

Baked apples or pears

Use baked apple recipe from Tuesday, Week One (page 67).

Variation: Pears, peaches, or plums can be substituted for apples.

Corn muffins or bread

1 six ounce box corn muffin mix
2/3 cup milk
1 egg, lightly beaten

Preheat oven to 400° F. Grease muffin tins. Place corn bread mix in bowl. Crack and lightly beat egg with fork, until yolk and white have been blended. Add milk, and mix. Batter will be lumpy. Bake for 10 to 12 minutes until muffins are done.

Variation: For corn bread instead of muffins, use a greased 8 inch by 8 inch metal baking pan, or a 9 inch round cast iron frying pan, greased. Baking time may be slightly longer.

Tip: Most corn bread mixes contain sugar. An alternate recipe for corn bread without sugar follows:

If you have time, and you want to make corn bread from scratch, use this recipe, which calls for white or yellow corn meal, available at most supermarkets, and baking powder, found in the baking supplies section of most supermarkets.

"Scratch" corn bread

1/4 cup vegetable oil or shortening, such as Crisco®.
1 cup yellow or white corn meal
1 cup all-purpose flour
1 Tbs. baking powder
1/2 tsp. salt (omit salt if you wish)
1 cup milk
1 egg, beaten

Preheat oven to 425° F. Melt vegetable shortening and use it to coat bottom of skillet or baking pan, reserving the rest. Combine the corn meal, flour, baking powder, and salt. Add the milk and egg;and mix. Add the remainder of the melted shortening and mix again. Pour into the skillet and bake 20 to 25 minutes or until a knife or toothpick inserted into the center of the corn bread comes out clean.

Lunch

Yogurt, fresh fruit, such as apples, pears or bananas, bread sticks, iced tea.

Variations: This lunch can be quite refreshing. You can substitute strawberries, cherries, orange sections or other seasonal fruit, as you wish.

Snack

Peanuts, cola drink, seedless grapes

About Peanuts

Peanuts are sold in several ways. There are the traditional salted peanuts that have been roasted in oil. Peanuts are also sold in the shell, and these have less salt and calories than roasted, salted peanuts. There are dry roasted peanuts that contain no added oil; and there are dry roasted peanuts sold without salt. All peanuts, even dry roasted unsalted peanuts are fairly high in calories. On the other hand, they are nutritious and taste good.

Dinner

English muffin pizzas, green salad, red wine, coffee or tea, Italian lemon ice or lemon sorbet

English muffin pizzas

four ounces shredded mozzarella cheese
sixteen ounce can tomato sauce
2 TBS tomato paste (optional)
2 TBS olive oil (use more or less as desired)
1/4 tsp. oregano
1/8 tsp. basil
dash ground hot red pepper (optional)
1 ounce cheddar cheese shredded, to taste (optional)
Parmesan cheese for sprinkling on pizzas
four English muffins, split
3 or 4 green onions chopped, or 1/2 medium onion, chopped

Preheat oven to 425° F. Split the English muffins. Sprinkle 1/8 of the mozzarella cheese on each of the eight muffin halves. If using tomato paste, mix with tomato sauce; if not, use 1/8 of the sauce on each of the muffin halves. Sprinkle basil, oregano and ground red pepper on the pizzas, and top with some of the olive oil. Sprinkle some grated cheddar cheese on top, if desired. Bake on cookie sheet in 425° F. oven for 15 to 20 minutes or until cheese is bubbling. Remove from oven and sprinkle with Parmesan cheese.

Tossed green salad #III

Romaine lettuce
iceberg lettuce
fresh mushrooms
toasted croutons
1 six ounce jar marinated artichoke hearts
garlic clove, peeled and smashed with flat side of knife
olive or salad oil, to taste

Rub salad bowl with smashed garlic clove and discard garlic. Wash the lettuce, removing any brown spots, and pat dry with paper towels or use a salad spinner if you have one. Tear the lettuce (cutting with scissors or knife makes edges turn brown) into small pieces. Remove artichoke hearts from jar, reserving marinade and place artichoke hearts into salad. Reserve the marinade from the artichoke hearts. Toss with dressing.

Artichoke dressing

marinade from the jar of artichoke hearts
olive oil or salad oil, about 1 to 2 Tbs.
fresh parsley (dried parsley may be used

To the reserved marinade from the artichoke hearts, add a quantity of olive oil or salad oil, and some chopped fresh or dried parsley. Shake well, and toss into salad. (The artichoke marinade contains oil, vinegar and spices).

Italian lemon ice

Use commercial lemon ice or substitute lemon sorbet or sherbet. Garnish with fresh mint or strawberries.

Tuesday, Week Two

Breakfast

Scrambled eggs, breakfast potatoes, fruit juice, toast and butter, tea or coffee. Prepare the potatoes first, and the eggs last.

Potatoes and peppers

2 medium potatoes, washed and cut up (peeling not necessary)
1 green or red bell pepper
1 small to medium onion
fresh parsley, chopped
oil for frying
salt and pepper

Cut up onion and wash and core green or red bell pepper. Cut pepper. Heat oil in skillet and put onions in to saute over low heat. Add peppers next. While they are cooking, wash and slice up (peeling is optional) two medium to large potatoes. Turn heat up to medium. Place potatoes in skillet and saute, turning occasionally to make sure they do not stick to pan. Cooking time: about 20 minutes after adding the potatoes. Serves four.

Scrambled eggs

Use scrambled eggs recipe from Wednesday, Week One (page 75).

Garnish ideas

Scrambled eggs provide a good background for any of the following garnishes:

minced green onions
fresh parsley sprigs
tomato slices or cherry tomatoes
sliced black olives
shredded hard cheddar cheese
orange slices

Lunch

Sliced ham and tomato sandwich with mayonnaise on rye bread, fresh apple or pear, beverage.

Ham and tomato sandwiches

For each sandwich, use:

2 slices bread
1 or two slices ham
tomato slices
mayonnaise to taste

Spread bread with mayonnaise. Place ham on one slice of bread, top with tomatoes and second slice of bread. Divide, if you wish, and serve. Serves one. This recipe can be increased to serve more people.

Tip: Fresh vegetables and fruit, such as potatoes, carrots, zucchini, apples, pears, or grapes, should always be washed before use.

Snack

Stuffed celery. Celery stuffed with cream cheese.

Stuffed celery

1 or 2 ribs celery, washed and cut into 3-inch pieces
cream cheese, about 1 TBS per rib of celery

Fill celery pieces with cream cheese. If cream cheese is hard, mix with a small amount of milk.

Dinner

Poached fish, parsley potatoes, green beans, rolls and butter, white wine, chocolate pudding, coffee or tea.

Poached whitefish

1 pound whitefish filets or filets of other mild white fish, such as flounder or sole
1 medium onion, chopped; or 3 green onions, chopped
1 carrot, chopped
1 rib celery, chopped
chopped parsley for garnish
1 quart poaching liquid (recipe below); if additional liquid is needed, use water
butter for sauteing vegetables
pinch of herb for vegetable saute; oregano, basil or parsley

Poaching liquid

2 cups white wine
2 cups water

Mix liquids together.

Variation: substitute chicken or fish stock for the wine; or use 1 cup white wine and one cup stock.

Preheat oven to 375° F. Saute vegetables in about 2 TBS butter and the herb you have chosen, for about ten minutes. Meanwhile, place the filets in an open baking dish or dishes and prepare the poaching liquid. Place the fish in the baking dish and sprinkle the vegetables on the filets. Add poaching liquid to barely cover.

Poach in the oven until the translucent color of the filets has turned opaque. This can be from ten minutes, to one half hour, depending on whether the poaching liquid was hot or cold and whether the oven is "slow" or "fast." Check the fish every five minutes or so, in order to keep it from overcooking. Serves four.

Microwave version: Cover dish with waxed paper or plastic wrap. Leave a "vent" for the air to escape. Microwave for brief periods, (3 minutes first turn, 2 minutes each successive turn)rotating the dish 90° each time. Be sure fish is opaque in color before serving.

Heads up: if using a microwave oven for any purpose, be sure to cover any open dishes with waxed paper or plastic wrap. Leave some openings for steam to escape. This keeps the food from splattering all over the inside of the microwave.

Idea for leftovers: chop or flake whitefish, add chopped celery, onion, and mayonnaise and serve as a salad or in sandwiches.

Parsley potatoes

potatoes (see below)
fresh parsley, about 1 Tbs., chopped (dried parsley may be substituted)
butter

Wash and partially or wholly peel enough potatoes to serve four people (three or four large; four or five medium; or six to eight small potatoes). If using large or medium potatoes, cut up. Place in pot with enough water to cover potatoes and boil for about 20 minutes, or until a fork stuck into a potato indicates the potatoes are done. Drain, and add small amount of butter, and fresh chopped parsley. Toss the potatoes in the butter and parsley.

Tip: What's that? You don't have *time* to peel potatoes? Here are a few alternative approaches:

1) *Don't peel them.* Wash them thoroughly and remove any "eyes" or blemishes; then cut them up with their skins still on, and proceed as above. Tell the diners the skins contain valuable vitamins and fiber (they do).

2) *Partially peel them.* Peel a strip around the middle of the potato. This looks very interesting and brightens up the presentation.

3) *Open a can of whole or sliced white potatoes.* Drain, then rinse under cold water (gets rid of starchy "canned" taste. Sprinkle the parsley on a flat surface Roll the potatoes (if whole) or lay them (if sliced) in or on the chopped parsley so each piece is lightly coated with parsley flakes. Warm up and serve.

Green beans

Prepare some frozen green beans. Use the green beans recipe from Monday, Week One (page 65).

Cheesecake

Use frozen commercial cheesecake; or use the following recipes.

Graham cracker crust

1 graham cracker pie crust (buy one at the store in its own pie plate, and already cooked); or use:

1 cup graham crackers, mashed
1 stick butter;

Mix ingredients well, and form into crust in a pie plate. Bake at 350° F. for ten minutes.

Never bake cheese cake

1 three ounce package cream cheese, softened to room temperature
1 tsp lemon juice
1 tsp vanilla extract
1/2 cup sugar
1/2 pint heavy cream, whipped (or use frozen whipped topping)
1 can fruit pie filling (cherry, apple, blueberry, strawberry)

Make certain the cream cheese has been softened, for easy mixing. Mix cream cheese, lemon juice, vanilla extract and sugar together (use an electric mixer, or cream well using a fork) and gently fold whipped cream into cream cheese mixture. Place in pie crust in pie plate (if you are using a pie crust that has to be baked, bake it first, and cool it, then add the cheesecake mixture. Chill in refrigerator eight hours or overnight. Store covered in refrigerator. Top with the pie filling just before serving. Serves six.

Wednesday, Week Two

Breakfast

Beer coffee cake, blueberries, orange juice, coffee or tea.

Beer coffee cake

The alcohol evaporates during baking. And the cake is good.

3 cups biscuit mix
1 twelve ounce can beer, preferably at room temperature
1/2 cup sugar
1 egg, beaten well with fork
1/2 stick butter, cut into small pieces
1 Tbs. cinnamon
1 tsp. vanilla
1/8 tsp. salt
confectioners sugar for topping
additional cinnamon for topping

Preheat oven to 350° F. Mix biscuit mix, butter, sugar, salt, cinnamon together; then add egg, vanilla, and beer and mix together in bowl and pour into greased 9 inch x 13 x 2 inch baking pan. Bake about 45 min, or until knife inserted into center of coffee cake comes out clean. Mix small amount (1 tsp.) of cinnamon with about 2 Tbs. confectioners sugar and dust cake with confectioners sugar. (This cake can be made the night before and stored in covered container or in refrigerator in covered dish.)

Tip: Baking tends to be more exacting than other kinds of cooking. Baking mix yields the best results when it is mixed well, but not *over mixed*. Put it in the oven as soon as all ingredients are mixed together. Some other kinds of batters, such as cornbread batter, need to "rest" for a few minutes before being put into the oven.

Variation: prepare recipe as above, and when cake has cooled slice horizontally, to make two layers. Fill with sliced peaches, replace top layer, and serve.

Idea for leftovers: serve beer coffee cake with ice cream; or, split, toast and butter and serve topped with strawberries.

Lunch

Corned beef hash, poached eggs

Corned beef hash

1 can corned beef (8 to 12 ounces)
3 or 4 leftover medium potatoes, or 3 or 4 potatoes boiled for this purpose
1/2 medium onion, chopped
1/4 cup green pepper, chopped
parsley chopped, to taste
salt and pepper

Break up corned beef. Combine with potatoes, onion, bell pepper, parsley and salt and pepper and form into patties. Saute over medium heat, turning once, until both sides are crisp. Serves four.

Rapid corned beef hash

Use one 15-1/2 ounce can corned beef hash; form into four patties; garnish with parsley. Fry over medium heat, turning once.

Poached eggs

4 eggs
about 1 tsp. salad oil or olive oil

Fill a frying pan or large saucepan with water to a depth of 1-1/2 to 2 inches. Heat to just below boiling. Spread 1 tsp. salad oil on a saucer. One at a time, remove eggs from shells and place on the saucer; then slide the egg into the hot water. Cook to taste, but at least until whites are opaque. As the white of the egg gets opaque a very thin film forms over the yolk. This is desirable. Remove the eggs in the same order they went into the pan using a large skimmer or turner. Place atop corned beef hash patties.

Variation: use fried eggs or soft boiled eggs.

Garnish ideas

sliced red radishes
chopped red pepper
mushroom slices

Tip: one way to get the water to just below boiling is to bring the water to a boil, then reduce the heat slightly.

Alternate serving suggestion: eggs can also be placed on plain or buttered toast or on English muffins.

Snack

Cucumber rounds with sour cream dollops, iced tea

Cucumber rounds with sour cream dollops

one cucumber, washed.
sour cream (or yogurt), about 3 or 4 Tbs.
garnish

It can be peeled, as well, if you wish; or it can be partially peeled by peeling a strip of skin off, then leaving some skin, peeling another strip off, and so forth, until there is a striped effect. Slice cucumber into slices about 1/8 to 1/4 of an inch thick. Place on tray and add dollop of sour cream to each slice. Garnish with parsley, red caviar, pieces of red or green pepper, or olive slices. Serves one or two. This recipe can be increased to serve more people.

Tip: this recipe also makes a great hors d' ouevre.

Dinner

Whole roasted chicken, curried rice, green peppers and zucchini, bread and butter, white wine, sorbet and blueberries.

Roasted chicken

Roasting is a really delicious way to prepare meats, fish, poultry and vegetables. While the food is roasting, the cook has time to take care of other tasks. This recipe sounds like a lot of work, but it really isn't. You will need about two hours for this meal. Preparation time is one-half hour. Roasting time is 90 minutes.

1 whole chicken, about 2 and 1/2 pounds to 3 and 1/2 pounds
4 or 5 small onions or two medium onions
fresh parsley
1 bay leaf
1 clove garlic, peeled
1/2 cup (or so) water (for sauce; recipe follows)
salt
pepper
small amount of butter, olive oil or salad oil, to rub on chicken and for basting

Preheat oven to 450° F. Remove chicken from packaging, rinse in cold water, then pat dry with paper towels. Rub bird all over with a little oil or butter. This assures a well-browned chicken.

Place in roasting pan or in cast iron frying pan, legs up. Peel the onions; rub the cavities of the chicken with about 1/4 tsp. of salt and not more than 1/4 tsp black pepper. Place the bay leaf, the parsley, and one of the onions in the large chicken cavity. Using kitchen twine, tie the legs together (if you don't have kitchen twine, the chicken will not look as neat but this is not fatal to the meal). Heat the butter or the oil in the frying pan, or melt the butter in a sauce pan.

Surround the chicken with the onions. Place in oven and baste about every ten minutes. Roast for about 1 hour to 1 and 1/2 hours, depending on your oven. Pierce the chicken (use the thickest part of the thigh) with a fork to test for doneness. The juices from the inside of the chicken should be clear (if they are pink, the chicken needs more cooking). Let chicken "rest" for about five or ten minutes after removing from the oven. Serves four.

Tip: you'll need pot holders and a long-handled spoon, if you have one, for this recipe. A carving fork and knife are also useful.

Heads up: when handling poultry, keep the area clean; do not let anything touched by the raw poultry, such as utensils, counter tops, or dishes, come into contact with anything else until the object touched by the poultry has been washed.

Sauce for roasted chicken

pan liquids
1 Tbs. flour

Place liquids in roasting pan, juices from chicken, and 1/2 cup water in frying pan; or, if you have used the frying pan to roast the chicken, remove chicken from frying pan and leave the juices; add the water. Scrape up any brown bits and pieces from the bottom of the pan and stir into the sauce. Add 1 Tbs. flour. Heat, stirring constantly, for a few minutes, until the water, flour, and the juices and pan drippings have become sauce. Spoon over chicken and serve with curried rice and a green vegetable.

Idea for leftovers: debone chicken, chop, and use in sandwiches.

Curried rice

1 cup white rice
1 small onion, peeled and chopped
1 Tbs. butter
1/8 tsp. salt (optional)
2 and 1/2 cups water
1/2 tsp. curry powder

Melt butter in 1 and 1/2 quart saucepan. Saute onion in butter until onion is soft but not brown. Add rice and and briefly saute. Add water and bring to full rolling boil over high heat. Cover saucepan and reduce heat to low. Let rice steam for about 20 minutes or until done. Just before removing rice, add curry powder and mix to coat rice. Four servings.

Tip: A little curry powder goes a long way. Some folks enjoy a more powerful curry taste, so start with a little and experiment with different amounts each time you prepare this recipe, until you find the level of curry flavor that you enjoy best.

Low-salt alternative: salt can be deleted from this recipe for those who do not wish it.

Green peppers and zucchini

1 small onion
2 zucchini
1 or 2 medium green peppers
olive oil to taste
1/2 cup water

Wash vegetables and peel onion. Slice zucchini and peppers; cut onion into pieces. Saute onions in saucepan with small amount of olive oil over medium heat about five minutes until onion has softened. Add vegetables and water and cover. Cook over medium heat until done (peppers will change to a soft green color and zucchini will be soft; onion will be translucent). Serves four.

Thursday, Week Two

Breakfast

   Cold cereal, bananas or blueberries, juice, toast, coffee or tea

Lunch

Hot dogs, buns, sauerkraut, mustard, relish, fruit, cola drink.

Hot dogs and sauerkraut

4 hot dogs or frankfurters
1 can sauerkraut (8 ounces or 16 ounces)

Steam or grill the hot dogs. In a saucepan, warm up sauerkraut. Serve with franks, buns, mustard and relish. (Serves two.)

Snack

Potato chips, iced tea

Dinner

Three cheese macaroni, orange, strawberry and onion salad, Ida's apple dessert, coffee, tea

Three cheese macaroni

1 box macaroni and cheese mix (about 7.5 to 10 ounces)
1/4 cup shredded mozzarella cheese
Parmesan cheese for sprinkling
butter (for macaroni and cheese mix)
milk (for macaroni and cheese mix)

Use box of packaged macaroni and cheese mix and follow directions on package. Blend cheese mixture into hot macaroni, adding the 1/4 cup shredded mozzarella cheese. Sprinkle with Parmesan cheese before serving. Serves two as main dish, four as side dish.

Ida's apple dessert

Eight or nine apples, washed and cored
1 tsp. cinnamon
3/8 cup brown sugar
2 tsp. lemon juice
1/4 to 1/2 cup water

Preheat oven to 350° F. Wash and core and slice about eight or nine apples. Place slices in 9 inch x 9 inch baking dish, in rows. Sprinkle with sugar, cinnamon, lemon juice, and water. Add crumbly topping (recipe follows), then bake 45 minutes to 1 hour. Serves six to eight.

Crumbly Topping

1/2 tsp. cinnamon
3/8 cup brown sugar, divided
2 Tbs. baking mix
1 Tbs. butter

Mix well together with back of fork, sprinkle over unbaked apples.

Idea for leftovers: serve Ida's apple dessert with ice cream.

Friday, Week Two

Breakfast

Cantaloupe, cottage cheese, fruit juice, toast or muffin, coffee or tea.

This is another meal where specific recipes aren't needed. Cut up the cantaloupe, place the cottage cheese in a small dish, serve the juice, breads and hot beverage, and enjoy the meal.

Lunch

Leftovers: macaroni and cheese, mixed with sliced hot dogs; celery sticks, bell pepper rings, bread or rolls, butter, soft drink.

Macaroni and cheese with sliced hot dogs

2 to 4 hot dogs; or leftover hot dogs from previous lunch
leftover macaroni and cheese

Slice hot dogs into 1/2 inch slices and briefly saute. Add leftover macaroni and cheese and warm up with hot dogs. Stir together and serve.

Celery sticks and bell pepper rings

1 rib celery
1 red or green bell pepper

Wash celery and split lengthwise. Cut into 3 inch sticks. Wash and core pepper. Slice into rings. Serves one to four. Use additional vegetables for more servings.

Snack

Cheese and crackers, soft drink.

Alternative snack--apple and small bag of potato chips.

Dinner

Easy eggplant bake, green salad, bread and butter, orange slices

Easy eggplant bake

2 cups bread cubes, about 1/2 inch x 1/2 inch. Bread can be slightly stale, or it can be toasted lightly in the oven
1 medium eggplant, peeled and diced into 1/2 inch x 1/2 inch cubes
2 medium onions, sliced crosswise then broken into rings
2 medium zucchini, sliced on the diagonal
2 medium tomatoes, sliced crosswise
oil and/or butter for sauteing
2 cups chicken broth or vegetable stock

Preheat oven to 375° F. In a skillet melt butter (if using) and add oil; heat but do not let the fat smoke. Gently saute the bread cubes about five minutes. Add the eggplant cubes and continue to saute for another five minutes. Do not let bread or eggplant burn. Place bread cube/eggplant mixture in a 9 x 13 x 2 inch baking dish. Layer zucchini, onions, and tomatoes on bread/eggplant mixture. Pour stock over dish. Bake in oven for about one hour. Serves six to eight.

Idea for leftovers: serve for lunch with tomato and onion salad.

Green salad with shrimp

Salad greens
4 ounces cocktail shrimp (sold in cans or jars, or frozen)
French or Russian dressing

Make your favorite green salad. Toss tiny cocktail shrimp in with the salad greens and serve with bottled French Russian dressing. If the shrimp is packed in cocktail sauce, add a little lemon juice and use the sauce on the salad. Otherwise, use bottled dressing.

Saturday, Week Two

Breakfast

Hot cereal, grapes, fruit juice, toast, coffee or tea

Prepare your favorite hot cereal according to package directions. . Wash grapes, pour the juice, butter the toast and serve.

Lunch

Pasta with cottage cheese and spinach, tomato wedges, bread, red wine.

Pasta with cottage cheese and spinach

1/2 pound macaroni, such as penne, or other pasta
1 ten ounce package frozen *chopped* spinach
1 eight ounce container cottage cheese, regular or low-fat
Parmesan cheese for sprinkling on pasta
salt and pepper (optional)

Cook pasta according to package directions. While pasta is boiling, place the frozen spinach into the pasta water. It will thaw and cook with the pasta. When ready. drain, and toss with 1 cup (8 ounces) regular or low fat cottage cheese. Sprinkle with Parmesan cheese. Serves four.

Snack

Banana and cookies or brownie, iced tea

Dinner

Meatloaf # II, green peas, potatoes, biscuits, rice pudding, coffee or tea.

Meatloaf # II

Preparation time is about 1/2 hour and cooking time is about 60 to 75 minutes.

2 pounds ground chuck or 1 pound ground chuck, 1/2 pound ground pork, 1/2 pound ground veal
1 large onion, chopped
1 green pepper, chopped
2 ribs celery, chopped
1 egg, lightly beaten
1 and 1/2 cups bread crumbs
1/8 tsp oregano
1/8 tsp thyme (or, skip the herbs and use seasoned bread crumbs)
1/4 cup chopped fresh parsley or 1 Tbs. dried parsley
1 can condensed cream of mushroom or cream of chicken soup
1/4 soup can water
1/4 soup can wine (or use 1/2 soup can water)
1 six ounce can tomato paste

Preheat oven to 350 f.° Chop vegetables and mix with ground meat loaf mix and bread crumbs. Add egg, a little at a time; add soup a little at a time; mix all ingredients well. Mixture will be fairly moist. Form into two long loaves and bake for 60 to 75 minutes or until meat loaves are done. Use a 9 x 13 x 2 inch baking dish. If using a meat loaf mixture containing pork, cook slightly longer. Serves eight, or two meals for four people.

Idea for leftovers: serve heated meat loaf sliced, along with mashed potatoes and gravy (use a jar of commercial brown gravy).

Idea for leftovers: reheat and slice the meat loaf and serve with rice, sauteed green peppers and tomato sauce.

Sunday, Week Two

Breakfast

1/2 grapefruit, oatmeal, toast, coffee or tea

Grapefruit

1 grapefruit

Cut grapefruit in half, run knife along lines separating sections in each half, and serve. Serves two.

Tip: Leftover grapefruit keeps well in the refrigerator for a day or two. Cover with waxed paper or plastic wrap.

Lunch

Deviled ham, sharp cheddar cheese and green pepper sandwich on whole wheat bread.

Deviled ham sandwiches

For each two sandwiches, you will need:
1 can deviled ham
1 green pepper, minced
sandwich spread
four bread slices

Deviled ham is ground ham mixed with spices and seasonings. It is sold in 4 ounce cans in supermarkets. Or chop leftover ham and mix it with a little onion and mustard. Spread bread slices with mustard or mayonnaise. Spread ham on one slice of the bread and top with pepper rings. Top with second slice of bread. Serves two.

Time-saver: use store-bought ham salad instead of deviled ham.

Idea for leftovers: use any leftover bell pepper rings as a snack. Use leftover deviled ham on crackers.

Snack

Coffee cookies with easy coffee frosting, hot drink. These cookies can be prepared the night before you use them for a snack.

Coffee cookies

1/2 cup solid shortening
2/3 cup sugar
2 Tbs. instant coffee
1 egg, slightly beaten
3/4 cup flour, sifted
1/8 tsp. salt
1/2 tsp vanilla extract

Preheat oven to 350°F. Cream together shortening, sugar, instant coffee. Add egg, flour, salt, vanilla and mix well. Place in teaspoons on greased cookie sheet. Bake for about 12 minutes. Remove from cookie sheet immediately. Makes 36 cookies.

Coffee frosting

1 cup sifted confectioners (powdered) sugar
2 TBS milk
1/2 tsp. instant coffee.

Mix until smooth and frost cookies.

Hors d'ouevre

Cucumber rounds with sour cream and caviar.

Cucumber rounds with sour cream and caviar

1 or 2 cucumbers
1/2 cup sour cream
1 2 ounce jar red or black lumpfish caviar

Wash cucumber. Using a potato peeler or paring knife, peel strips off cucumbers lengthwise, so that unpeeled strips alternate with peeled strips. Slice cucumbers crosswise into 1/4 inch or thinner slices. Place cucumber rounds on flat surface. Add a dollop of sour cream to each cucumber round and place a small amount of caviar on each round. The yield will be approximately 32 or more cucumber rounds, depending upon size of cucumbers and thickness of slices.

Note: lumpfish caviar is a fairly inexpensive caviar that is frequently used in canapes and hors d'ouevres. It is found in the gourmet sections of supermarkets. There are many varieties and grades of caviar, and the top end can be expensive, indeed. For an hors d'ouevres or appetizers, use the everyday varieties.

Low fat, low salt alternative: use fat free sour cream or nonfat yogurt; substitute small pieces of red bell pepper for the caviar.

Dinner

Oven pot roast and vegetables, endive and romaine salad with Beth's dressing, orange slices or carrot cake, coffee or tea.

Oven pot roast and vegetables

1 two-pound chuck roast, boneless. (If using a bone-in roast, use one about 1/2 pound larger
4 medium potatoes, scrubbed and diced (peeling them is optional)
1 carrot, diced
1 rib celery, diced
2 medium onions, chopped
1 envelope dry onion soup mix
1 bottle (750 ml.) dry red wine (inexpensive is okay)
1 bay leaf
1/8 cup fresh parsley, chopped or 1 TBS dried parsley
olive oil
black pepper, to taste
1 pinch rosemary
1 pinch thyme

Preheat oven to 350°F. Place olive oil in frying pan and heat; brown beef on all sides over medium flame (this will occur fairly quickly). Remove beef and place in four quart covered casserole. Place potatoes, carrot, celery, and onions in casserole and saute briefly, stirring thoroughly, so that each vegetable piece is lightly oiled. Place vegetables in casserole around beef, adding spices and mixing well. Add wine to casserole, and sprinkle the onion soup mix over the roast and vegetables.

Cover casserole and place in oven; bake for one and 1/2 to two hours or until potatoes and carrots are soft when pierced with a fork. (No salt is needed for this recipe, since there is plenty of salt in the onion soup mix.) Serves six to eight, with leftovers.

Endive and romaine salad with Beth's dressing

12 leaves endive, washed and broken up
six leaves romaine, washed and broken up
two medium tomatoes, cut into pieces (or 12 cherry tomatoes)

Toss greens with tomatoes and serve with Beth's dressing (recipe below). Serves six.

Beth's dressing

3 Tbs. olive oil or other salad oil
1 Tbs. balsalmic vinegar
1 Tbs. brown sugar

Dissolve sugar in vinegar and add to olive oil; mix well and toss with salad.

Orange slices

Peel two oranges, removing the white part under the skin. Slice, drizzle with brandy or liqueur.

Carrot cake

Buy a frozen carrot cake, defrost and serve. Or, make one, using a cake mix, and follow directions on box. Carrot cakes usually have a cream cheese frosting; these can be purchased ready made as well. Or, if you have the time and equipment, make the cake and frosting from scratch, using the recipes below:

Carrot cake

4 eggs
1 and 1/2 cups granulated sugar
3/4 cup olive oil or salad oil
1/4 cup orange juice or lemon juice (lemon juice will make the cake more tart)
1 tsp. vanilla extract ← *
2 tsp. cinnamon, ground
1 and 1/2 tsp. baking soda
1 tsp. baking powder
1/2 tsp. salt (optional)
2 cups carrots, shredded (shred to about the size seen in cole slaw)
1/4 cup raisins, chopped (optional)
butter, for greasing cake pans
flour, for greasing cake pans

You will need two 9-inch round cake pans and two wire cake racks. Preheat oven to 350° F. Grease and flour cake pans. Using an electric mixer at medium speed, a whisk or an egg beater, beat the eggs, granulated sugar, olive oil, orange juice, and vanilla until mixed well. Beat in the flour, cinnamon, baking soda, baking powder and salt, until well mixed. Add the shredded carrots, and the chopped raisins, if you are using them, stirring gently until the carrots have been well distributed throughout the batter. Place half of the batter in each of the two cake pans.

Bake for about 30 minutes, or until a knife blade inserted in the middle of the cake comes out clean. Place the cake pans on the wire racks for five or six minutes, to cool. Run a knife blade around the inside of each cake pan. Turn the cakes out onto the wire racks to cool further. When the cakes have cooled to room temperature, frost with cream cheese frosting.

Page 12

* In the in

Cream cheese frosting

1 eight ounce package of cream cheese, at room temperature
one pound of confectioners sugar (powdered sugar)
1 to 2 tsps. milk, to adjust the consistency of the frosting
1 tsp. vanilla extract
raisins, for garnish

  Using an electric mixer or a fork, beat the confectioners sugar into the cream cheese, adding the vanilla. Slowly add milk, as necessary, until the frosting is a good consistency to spread. Use about 1/3 of the frosting to cover the first layer, and 1/3 to cover the second layer. Place one layer on top of the other. Using the remaining frosting, coat the sides of the cake. Garnish with raisins.

Chapter Six

Stocking Up, Week Three

FIRST, take inventory. Do you need to replace any of the "Always Theres"™? What perishables are left from the first two weeks? Can some of them be used? For example, if there are bananas left over, they can be used as snacks; or on cereal; or served with ice cream or sliced onto pudding or gelatin; or peeled, chopped, and frozen for later use in banana bread. Once you've gone through what you have on hand, you can check the menus and recipes and decide what you will need. Items to be used in this week's menus include:

Dairy products

Cream: for whipping. Most stores sell a product in the dairy case called whipping cream, which can be whipped with a wire wisk, a mechanical egg beater, or an electric mixer. Aerosol cans of whipped topping or cartons of frozen whipped topping are a good substitute.

Eggs: one dozen

Cheese: cheddar, as needed;

Cottage cheese, or ricotta: 16 ounce package, or more, as needed;

Mozzarella: shredded, 8 ounces

Milk: as needed

Yogurt: as needed

Butter or margarine, as needed

Meat and Fish

Bacon: 1/2 to 1 pound (if you have some left from last week, use that up first).

Ground beef: 2 pounds; or 1 pound ground beef, and 1/2 pound each ground pork and ground veal

Chicken: one frying chicken, cut up into pieces

Boneless pork roast: Typically, these weigh anywhere from 2 to 3 and 1/2 pounds. Pork roast makes great leftovers. If you prefer, you can substitute a veal roast of the same size.

Sliced ham: about 4 ounces for each serving, or 1 slice ham steak; or 1 four ounce can deviled ham (each can serves one or two).

Sliced bologna: about 4 ounces for each serving.

Scallops: about 1/4 pound for each serving.

Sausage links, 8 ounces: These can be pork or turkey sausage.

Produce

Take inventory to see what produce is left from last week, and its condition. Buy what you need of the following items. Remember, some types of produce, such as apples, cabbage, carrots, onions and potatoes keep well for some time. Bell peppers, celery, and green beans can be stored in the refrigerator, but are best used within a few days or a week. Cucumbers and bananas don't store well, and should be used fairly soon after they are purchased.

Apples: as needed

Bananas: as needed

Celery: one stalk

Mushrooms, fresh: about eight ounces.

Onions: as needed. If you have onions left from last week, it is fun to try a different kind of onion. Maybe the long green onions called scallions; or one of the purple onions that are good in salads.

Oranges: three or four

Pears: four (or 1 can pear halves or 1 package frozen pears). Other good kinds of tree fruit to consider buying are nectarines, peaches, apricots, and plums. Also, pears themselves come in several varieties. Try a variety you didn't buy last time.

Potatoes: as needed. If you have previously tried russet (Idaho) potatoes, try a new variety, such as redskin or Yukon gold.

Strawberries: one pint to one quart. Are you a big fruit eater? You might also like to try a carton of blueberries.

Tomatoes: two or three medium

Cherry tomatoes: one pint. These are for an hors d'ouevre. They are also good in salads and as a garnish.

Watermelon: Ask the produce manager how much to buy. Many stores sell watermelon already cut up. Modest servings would be about 1/4 pound per person, more generous servings about 1/2 pound per person. Some of the melon is rind and is not eaten.

Frozen (or fresh) products

Spinach: one 10 ounce package frozen chopped spinach

Ice cream or frozen yogurt: buy as much as you think you're going to need. Generally, a pint serves two to four people).

Fruit juice: Check on your juice supply and replenish it, if necessary.

Frozen waffles: Again, how many to buy depends on how many people you are feeding and what their appetites are like. If you're just one or two people, six are usually enough. For more servings, figure three or four waffles per person for hearty appetites, and two to three for more modest appetites.

Brussels sprouts, one 10 ounce box: Frozen Brussels sprouts are pretty good, and don't have to be washed. Fresh Brussels sprouts are okay, too, if you find them, and prefer them.

Parsley, one bunch, as needed.

Tip: Are you using enough parsley? It's great to decorate a plate, or garnish a soup. It's good, added to a salad, or sprinkled on potatoes or rice.

Whipped topping: If you are not going to purchase whipping cream, get an aerosol can of whipped topping from the dairy case or a carton of whipped topping from the frozen foods section.

Staples

Pretzels or pretzel sticks: one bag. Pretzels and other snacks are an item of personal choice. Let your eating patterns be your guide on what, and how much, to buy.

Popcorn: There are many varieties of popcorn on the market, flavored, microwave, etc. Popcorn can be cooked in a corn popper, or in a large covered pot. Follow package directions. If you're not into popping your own, buy some popcorn already popped.

Pancake or waffle syrup, or corn syrup: How's the pancake (or waffle) syrup holding out? If you still have some, it's fun to try a different type, such as maple syrup, molasses, or light or dark corn syrup.

Canned foods

If you're going to be using canned deviled ham, blueberry topping, or canned pears, be sure to get these instead of comparable fresh items.

Juice, fruit or vegetable. You might want to try vegetable juice as a snack item. It is sold in many sizes in jars or cans.

Low salt alternative: supermarkets carry low-sodium vegetable juice.

Cream of mushroom soup, two cans. Remember, canned condensed cream of mushroom soup is virtually interchangeable with cream of chicken, cream of celery, cream of turkey, and cream of asparagus soup. Over time, try all of these varieties, and you'll discover that you may prefer one kind over another).

Tuna, one or two 6.5 or 7 ounce cans.

White kidney beans (or great Northern or cannelini beans), one 15 ounce can.

Dried foods

Check your supplies. Spices, seasonings, breakfast cereals, crackers--what's there, and what do you need?

Pasta, one pound for each eight servings. You might want to try "bow tie" pasta if you can find it. While different shapes of pasta may be more well suited to one or another kind of sauce, pasta is a very forgiving menu item. So, if you can't find bow tie pasta, try shells, elbows, or even plain spaghetti.

Powdered sugar, one 8 or 16 ounce package.

Paprika., one small jar or can. This spice is used to add flavor and color to cooked foods. It is especially good on chicken, or on egg salads.

Baked goods

English muffins, one package

Bread, one pound. How's your bread supply? Do you have some started bread stored in the freezer? Use some of it this week and purchase a different variety. One good use for bread that is still okay but no longer absolutely fresh is French toast; another is sandwiches, since mayonnaise or mustard will moisten the bread somewhat.

Chapter Seven

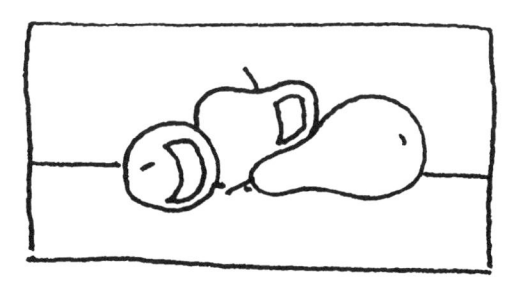

Menus and Recipes for Week Three

MORE COMPLICATED, but more satisfying. You've roasted and baked, boiled and fried. On to some recipes slightly more complex, and some good looking presentations, and some really great meals!

Week Three menus:

Monday

Breakfast: Baked pears, English muffins, butter, jelly, coffee, tea, or milk

Lunch: Ham salad sandwiches on whole wheat bread, cream of chicken (or cream of mushroom) soup, lemonade

Snack: Celery sticks stuffed with cream/cheddar cheese mixture, mineral water.

Dinner: "Always there" pasta with butter sauce (alternative: Red Sauce II), pear grape and orange salad, red wine, coffee, Tiramisu II

Tuesday

Breakfast: Easy egg spinach bake, toast, fruit juice, coffee, tea, or milk.

Lunch: Leftover always there pasta and red sauce II, white bean salad, mineral water, apple

Snack: Vegetable juice, crackers

Dinner: Sauteed scallops, rice, asparagus spears, apple sauce, iced tea, cookies or brownie, coffee

Wednesday

Breakfast: Breakfast bake, strawberries, toast, muffins or rolls; coffee or tea

Lunch: BLT! Bacon, lettuce and tomato sandwich on roll or bread, orange, iced tea, candy bar

Snack: Mixed nuts, apple

Dinner: Hungarian golden chicken, oregano potatoes or rice, carrots, peas, lemonade or white wine.

Thursday

Breakfast: Fried eggs on English muffins or biscuits, ham, fruit juice, coffee or tea

Lunch: Leftover chicken served cold, green salad, lemonade, cookies

Snack: Popcorn (regular or microwave)

Dinner: Faux "fresh" cream of mushroom soup, tuna, rice and red pepper salad, leftover cake or ice cream

Friday

Breakfast: Cold cereal, toast, banana, fruit juice, coffee or tea

Lunch: Bologna, cheddar and tomato sandwich on hard roll

Snack: Strawberries, tea

Dinner: Pork roast, oven roasted potatoes, Brussels sprouts, bread and butter, coffee or tea, ice cream

Saturday

Breakfast: Waffles, blueberry topping, fruit juice, coffee or tea

Lunch: Roast pork and roasted red pepper sandwiches, iced tea or cola

Snack: Pretzel sticks, fruit juice

Dinner: Bacon burgers, rolls, baked beans, pickles, relish, catsup, mustard, hot potato salad, tomato slices, watermelon, soda pop or fruit punch

Sunday

Breakfast: Hot cereal, orange slices, toast, fruit juice, coffee or tea

Lunch: Egg salad sandwiches, pears, cookies, milk

Snack: Ice cream, coffee or cola drink

Hors d'ouevre: Stuffed cherry tomatoes

Dinner: Bow tie pasta with scallions, salmon and tomato, rolls, white wine, green salad, cantaloupe, coffee or tea

Monday, Week Three

Breakfast

Baked pears , English muffins, butter, jelly, milk, coffee, or tea.

Baked pears

Use baked apple recipe from Tuesday, Week One, and substitute pears for the apples.

Lunch

Ham sandwiches on whole wheat bread, cream of chicken soup, lemonade.

Ham (or other cold cut) sandwiches

For four sandwiches, you will need:

8 slices cooked ham (you can substitute about 8 ounces pork , chicken or other luncheon meat, such as Spam).
1 rib celery, finely chopped
1/2 medium onion, finely chopped
mayonnaise, to taste
eight whole wheat bread slices (substitute white or rye, if you wish)
ground black pepper, to taste

Mix all ingredients except the meat slices, and spread on one side of the whole wheat bread slices. Serves two to three.

Variations: tired of ham? You can use chicken, turkey, or tuna. Out of cooked meat? You can use a can of luncheon meat; or you can hard boil a couple of eggs (about one egg per person) and make egg salad sandwiches. This is where the Always Theres™ come in handy. Prefer f   or seafood? Substitute tuna, salmon or crab meat. Vegetarian? Use Swiss cheese instead of meat.

Cream of chicken soup

1 can condensed cream of mushroom soup
1 soup can milk
parsley leaves for garnish

Empty contents of soup can into saucepan and slowly add milk, stirring constantly. Heat but do not boil. Garnish with parsley flakes. Serves two to three.

Variations: there are low salt and low fat soups on the market, if you're watching salt or fat. There are many varieties of canned and dried soups. You might try cream of tomato, or potato; or a vegetable soup.

Snack

Celery sticks stuffed with cream/cheddar cheese mixture, mineral water.

Cream and cheddar cheese blend for stuffing

3 oz. cream cheese, at room temperature
2 oz. cheddar cheese, shredded
small amount milk (optional)

Using a fork, blend cheddar cheese into cream cheese. If mixture seems too stiff, blend in about 1 tsp. milk. Use to stuff celery.

Variation: use the cream and cheddar cheese blend on top of crackers.

Dinner

Always theres™ pasta with butter sauce (alternative: Red Sauce # II, grape, orange and pear salad, red wine, rolls, coffee or tea, and Tira Misu II

Make the Tira Misu II first. Prepare the salad while pasta water is heating up, or after you put the pasta in the oven

Butter Sauce

1/2 cup (1 stick) butter
1/4 cup olive oil
1 clove garlic, minced finely
1/2 cup fresh parsley, chopped

Heat butter and olive oil together in skillet; when butter is melted, add garlic and parsley. Toss with hot pasta.

Alternative sauce:

Always theres™ pasta with Red Sauce II

This recipe is fast, easy to prepare and tastes really good (kind of the hallmark of this book). While the pasta is baking, you can set the table, have a cocktail and watch the 7:00 news.

1/2 pound cooked penne or elbow macaroni
1 jar (one quart) pasta sauce
1 red bell pepper, cored and cut into bite sized pieces
1/2 cup red wine (from the bottle you're serving for dinner)
some pepperoni or salami if you have it around
1/2 pound ricotta or farmer's or cottage cheese, or cream cheese
fresh parsley to taste
Parmesan cheese for serving on spaghetti
salt and pepper, to taste

Preheat oven to 375°F. Cook the pasta, following directions on box. Drain. Meanwhile, heat the sauce, adding the red pepper, the wine and the pepperoni. If you're using cream cheese, cut it into small pieces and add it to the pasta. If you're using the ricotta cheese, farmer's cheese or cottage cheese, just spoon it from the carton onto the hot pasta.

Place half the hot pasta and cheese mixture into a 2 and 1/2 to 3 quart casserole dish. Cover with half the sauce. Repeat with a second layer of pasta, cheese and sauce. Sprinkle with parsley if desired. Place in preheated 375° F. oven for one hour. Serve with Parmesan cheese and rolls. Serves four.

Grape, orange and pear salad

1 bunch seedless grapes (red or green, red preferred)
2 oranges, peeled and white pith removed, and sliced
1 pear, cored and cut into eight pieces
simple oil and vinegar dressing, to taste
crumbled blue cheese (optional)

Arrange orange and pear slices on plates. Add some grapes to each plate. Red seedless grapes provide better contrast, if you can get them, but green work well, too. Pour a small amount of oil and vinegar dressing (recipe follows) over fruit. Crumble blue cheese on top. Serves four.

Simple oil and vinegar dressing

6 Tbs. olive oil or salad oil
2 Tbs vinegar

Mix well and pour on salad, just prior to serving. Toss and serve.

Tira Misu # II

This recipe uses pound cake, which you can purchase frozen or fresh. The filling is ricotta cream, and is easy to prepare.

4 pound cake slices, arranged together on dish
1 cup rum coffee (recipe follows)
1 cup ricotta cream (recipe follows)
1/2 cup whipped cream or whipped topping
1/2 cup chocolate syrup, such as Hershey's
1 tsp. cinnamon
1 tsp. cocoa powder

Assemble pound cake slices. Pour some of the rum coffee over each slice, until it is used up. Spread the ricotta cream over each slice. Top with whipped cream. Pour a small amount of chocolate syrup over the whipped cream for contrast. Dust with cinnamon and cocoa powder. Chill in refrigerator for one hour or more. Serves four. Can be expanded.

Rum coffee

1/4 cup rum
3/4 cup strong coffee (may be made from instant coffee, or you can use leftover coffee)

Mix rum and coffee together.

Ricotta cream

1 cup ricotta
3 Tbs. powdered sugar
2 Tbs. rum
1/8 tsp. nutmeg

Whip ricotta with wire whisk or with electric mixer. Blend in rum, powdered sugar, and nutmeg. Spread over pound cake slices.

Tuesday, Week Three

Breakfast

Easy spinach egg bake, toast, fruit juice, coffee, tea, or milk.

Easy spinach egg bake

1 package frozen chopped spinach
6 eggs
1 cup shredded Monterey Jack or mozzarella cheese
salt and pepper, to taste

Preheat oven to 375°F. Cook the spinach in a saucepan, with a small amount of water, or in the microwave. Drain and stir. Place loosely in six ramekins or six oven-proof cups. Make a small depression in each portion of spinach to receive the egg. Crack the eggs, and place one egg in each ramekin, over the spinach. The yolk will settle into the depression in the spinach and the white will slowly percolate into the spinach. Add salt and pepper. Sprinkle 1/6 of the cheese over each ramekin. Bake for 12 to 15 minutes, until whites are firm and cheese is bubbling. Serve with toast or English muffins. Serves six.

Low-fat variation: use nine egg whites and one egg yolk; beat the yolk into the whites; use low-fat cheese; eliminate the salt. The presentation will be less dramatic but it is still mighty good eating.

Low-salt variation: eliminate the salt. Add a pinch or two of thyme or rosemary.

Lunch

Leftover "always theres™" pasta with red sauce II, white bean salad, mineral water, apple.

White bean salad I

This is a simple salad that can be used at lunch or dinner, and served at room temperature or heated to be served slightly warm.

1 can white kidney beans (or other white beans)
1/4 cup chopped onion
1 garlic clove, minced (optional)
fresh chopped parsley, to taste
black pepper, to taste

Open can of white kidney beans (or great northern beans or canellini beans.) Rinse in colander and drain. Add 1/4 cup chopped onion, minced garlic (optional), and parsley and black pepper to taste. If you're using the garlic, be sure to use the parsley, which helps to balance the flavors. Toss gently with some olive oil. Serves two as a main dish or four as a side dish.

Variation: serve on lettuce leaves with sliced tomatoes.

Idea for leftovers: flake a can of tuna (drained first) into the leftover bean salad, for a main course dish (serves two) or side dish (serves four).

Snack

Vegetable juice, crackers

Dinner

Sauteed scallops, rice, asparagus spears, apple sauce, rolls, butter, iced tea, cookies or brownie, coffee.

Sauteed scallops

1 pound sea scallops or bay scallops
parsley
lemon
oil for sauteing
fresh parsley sprigs

Wash scallops, removing any shell or connective tissue. Place oil in skillet over medium heat. Saute scallops until they turn opaque. (They are translucent when raw.) Transfer to serving dish, sprinkle with parsley; serve with lemon wedges. Serves four.

Rice

You'll notice there are a number of rice recipes in this book. This one uses chicken stock, which yields a more savory rice than plain water, and complements the flavor of the scallops.

1 cup rice. (if using instant rice, follow package directions)
1 cup water and 1 cup chicken stock; or two cups water

Put rice and water into saucepan. Cover and bring to a boil. Reduce heat to low and simmer until rice is cooked, about 15 to 20 minutes for converted white rice. Serves four.

Asparagus spears

One pound asparagus spears
Salt (optional)

Wash asparagus, removing any woody bottoms. Place in skillet, cover with water or stock, and simmer until asparagus is tender, about 10 to 15 minutes. Serves four.

Variation: asparagus spears also come in cans. These are expensive, but they can be served uncooked, or simply warmed up.

Idea for leftovers. Cut up leftover asparagus spears and use them in an omelette.

Apple sauce

Open jar of apple sauce and serve with the dinner, or in small side ramekins or dishes.

Tip: apple sauce, technically a fruit, can do yeoman service as a vegetable, and requires no cooking. Many markets sell it in glass jars, which can be re-closed and stored in the refrigerator. If you've got separate little bowls, it can be served in them, adding a bit of lustre to the table setting. It benefits from a dash of cinnamon. If you enjoy apple sauce warm, it can be warmed up. If you like it cold, chill it. If you're in a rush, serve it at room temperature.

Healthy eating idea: apple sauce is also great as a low-fat dessert, alone, or with a dollop of non-fat yogurt on top. If you're watching your sugar intake, sugar-free apple sauce is available in many super markets. Most apple sauce is packed without added salt. Check the ingredients on the can or jar

Wednesday, Week Three

Breakfast

Breakfast bake, strawberries, toast or muffins, coffee or tea.

Breakfast bake

- four slices bread, cut into cubes
- one medium onion, chopped
- 3/4 cup milk (six ounces)
- four eggs, or one eight ounce carton egg substitute
- eight ounces pork or turkey sausage links
- four ounces cheddar or Monterey jack cheese (use low fat cheese if you wish)
- dash hot sauce

Saute sausages in small amount of fat and set aside; pour off most of the fat and saute the onions until they are soft. Place the bread cubes on the bottom of a 8 x 8 x 2 inch baking dish. Mix onions, cut up sausages, eggs, hot sauce, and milk together and pour over bread cubes. Add cheese. Refrigerate for one hour or overnight. Place in preheated 350° F. oven and bake for about one hour. Serves four to six.

Healthy eating idea: use egg substitute, turkey sausage, and low-fat milk for a version of this dish that is considerably lower in fat.

Lunch

Bacon, lettuce and tomato sandwich on whole wheat toast, ice tea, granola bar

Bacon, lettuce and tomato sandwich

- four slices bacon
- one tomato, sliced
- one slice lettuce
- two slices bread
- mayonnaise or low fat mayonnaise

Toast bread, spreading one side of each slice with mayonnaise. On one slice, lay down lettuce, top with tomato, then bacon. Cover with other slice, mayonnaise side down. Cut in halves or quarters and serve. Serves one.

Snack

Mixed nuts, fresh apple

Dinner

Hungarian golden chicken, parsley potatoes, carrots, peas, lemonade or white wine.

Hungarian golden chicken

1 chicken, cut up into eight pieces
vegetable oil, about 1/2 to 3/4 cup
fresh garlic clove, minced or garlic powder
paprika
1 or 2 medium onions, cut up

Preheat oven to 350° F. Rinse chicken in cold water, pat dry with paper towels. Place oil in skillet and saute onions; while onions are sauteing, place chicken pieces in pan and brown. Place in baking pan and sprinkle garlic pieces or powder over top; sprinkle paprika over top of chicken. Bake about 1 and 1/2 hours. Serves four.

Oregano potatoes

4 medium potatoes, washed and cut up
dried oregano
salt and pepper to taste

Wash and cut up potatoes (peeling is optional). Place in pot with cold water to cover potatoes by about one inch. Bring to boil and cook until potatoes are done (may be pierced easily with a fork). Sprinkle with fresh chopped parsley and season to taste.

Variation: after potatoes are cooked, coat with a small amount of melted butter, then sprinkle with rosemary instead of oregano.

Variation: use leftover rice instead of oregano potatoes. Or use a package of frozen French fries, prepared in the oven on a cookie sheet (follow package directions).

Peas and carrots

Use enough of the contents from a bag of frozen peas and carrots to serve four people (about two cups); or mix carrots and peas from separate containers. Heat in saucepan with a small amount of water until warmed through. Serves four.

Microwave: place vegetables in covered dish, with a small amount of water. Microwave for three minutes on high; rotate dish, microwave for two minutes on medium. Check for doneness; if needed, microwave for another one or two minutes. Serves four.

Variation: if you'd like a more elaborate carrot dish, try:

Carrots Csilla

(Csilla is pronounced "Chilla" and she is from a family of very good cooks.) Use frozen sliced carrots or wash and slice some fresh carrots. Use about 1 large carrot per person. Place some butter (about 1/4 of a stick, or a little less) in a skillet over low heat until it is sizzling; add carrots, stirring while they are heating.

Add about two Tbs. of molasses or a couple of Tbs of brown sugar and a small amount of water. Continue to stir until carrots are cooked, (you can put a fork through one easily), glazed and hot enough to serve. Optional--add a jigger of bourbon near the end of the cooking. Serves four.

Idea for leftovers: reheat chicken and serve with a green salad. Use any leftover vegetables in a soup or stew.

Thursday, Week Three

Breakfast

Fried eggs on English muffins or biscuits, fruit juice, coffee or tea.

Fried eggs

4 eggs
oil, butter or margarine, or bacon fat

Place fat in skillet and heat over medium heat. Break eggs into pan. Fry until whites are opaque. Serve "sunny side up" If eggs "over" are desired, use flat pancake turner to flip eggs just before serving. You'll find that you may break a few yolks, but you'll soon get the hang of it. Eggs with broken yolks taste fine, by the way.

Lunch

Leftover chicken, green salad, bread and butter, milk or lemonade, cookies.

Snack

Popcorn, regular or microwave varieties.

Popcorn

Popcorn is available in a number of forms, commercially. Very popular are home popcorn preparations, which can be made in a corn popper, a covered pot, or in a microwave oven. Select the type you want, and carefully follow the directions on the box to achieve good results.

Dinner

Surprising "fresh" mushroom soup, tuna rice and red pepper salad, cake or ice cream, coffee or tea.

Surprising "fresh" canned mushroom soup

This "faux" fresh mushroom soup is really good. The surprise is that this "fresh" soup begins life as canned condensed soup.

1 can condensed cream of mushroom soup
1 cup sliced fresh mushrooms
1/2 soup can milk
1/2 soup can water or chicken broth
small amount butter, (about 1/4 stick) for sauteing mushrooms
fresh parsley, chopped, with some reserved for garnish
1 tsp. sherry (optional)

Clean and slice mushrooms, and saute in butter using frying pan. While mushrooms are sauteing, slowly add milk, then water, to cream of mushroom soup, stirring constantly. Place in saucepan, then add mushrooms and liquid from saute process, then parsley, continuing to stir. Reserve some parsley for garnish. Add sherry (optional). When hot but not boiling, serve and garnish each bowl of soup with parsley sprig. Makes about 4 servings 5/8 cup each.

Tip: since canned condensed soups are high in salt content, no salt is needed for this recipe.

Tuna, rice and red pepper salad

This is an excellent and substantial cold salad that can be eaten in sandwiches or as a stand-alone main course.

2 six and 1/2 to seven ounce cans or one thirteen ounce can tuna fish.
1 sweet red bell pepper, chopped
1 medium onion, chopped
1 rib celery, chopped
1 cup cooked rice, preferably chilled
2 TBS mayonnaise
chopped fresh parsley, about 1/4 cup

Drain tuna and flake into bowl. Add red pepper, onion, celery, rice, and parsley; toss. Add mayonnaise and toss. Add black pepper to taste. Refrigerate if desired, for about one hour. Serves four.

Variations: use canned or leftover salmon, cooked chicken, ham, or canned luncheon meat instead of the tuna. Green bell pepper can be substituted for the red bell pepper.

Friday, Week Three

Breakfast

Cold cereal, toast, banana or plum, fruit juice, coffee or tea

Another breakfast that does not require elaborate preparation, but that is simple and tasty.

Lunch

Bologna, cheddar and tomato sandwich on hard roll, apple or nectarine, cola drink or mineral water.

Bologna, cheddar and tomato sandwich on hard roll

For each sandwich you will need:

2 slices bologna
1 hard roll
cheddar slices or single process cheese slices
tomato slices
mustard, mayonnaise or both
lettuce slice (optional)

Split hard roll and spread with mustard, mayonnaise (or one half with one, one half with the other); place bologna, then cheddar on roll half. Top with tomato slices and lettuce slice, if desired.

Snack

Strawberries, tea

Dinner

Roast pork and oven roasted potatoes, Brussels sprouts, bread and butter, ice cream or sherbet.

Roast Pork with oven roasted potatoes

1 two and 1/2 to 3 and 1/2 pound pork roast, rolled and tied.
sage, to taste
four potatoes, washed and cut into quarters
two medium onions, cut into pieces.
1 carrot, cut into pieces
1 rib celery, cut into pieces (optional)

Preheat oven to 400° F. Put 1 Tbs. olive oil or salad oil in a large bowl. Wash and cut up vegetables and potatoes (peeling optional), place in bowl and lightly coat each piece with the oil. Place roast in pan on rack, to allow fat to drip to bottom of pan. Place onions, potatoes, carrot, and celery, if used, around roast. Roast for one hour at 400°, then lower oven to 350° and continue roasting for about another 90 minutes, or until meat is done. Pork should be cooked more thoroughly than other meats. Serves 4 to 6.

Note: roasting without a rack yields a roast that is roasted on the top and actually sauteed (since it is in contact with the hot fat) on the bottom. This is not a bad thing, by any means. You decide.

Brussels sprouts

Brussels sprouts are a vegetable in the cabbage family, available fresh or frozen. They should be boiled until just tender, then served with butter. Serves four.

Microwave: if frozen, microwave for about six minutes, in covered dish, rotating dish once. If fresh, use covered dish and microwave for three minutes, rotate dish, and microwave for one minute longer. At this point, check for doneness. Microwave a bit longer, if needed. Serves four.

Healthy eating alternative: boil the Brussels sprouts in low-fat low salt chicken stock and serve with a little black pepper.

Saturday, Week Three

Breakfast

Waffles with blueberry topping, fruit or juice, coffee or tea.

Waffles with blueberry topping

frozen waffles, about 2 per person
fresh or frozen blueberries, about 1/4 cup per person

Prepare waffles according to directions on package. Top with blueberries. If using frozen blueberries, thaw them first.

Variation: use commercial blueberry topping or blueberry jam.

Lunch

Roast pork and red pepper sandwiches, iced tea or cola

Roast pork and red pepper sandwiches

For each two sandwiches, you will need:

Leftover pork roast, sliced
1 red pepper sliced into rings
lettuce
mayonnaise
bread of your choice

Spread bread with mayonnaise, and layer lettuce, pork slices, and red pepper rings. Top with second slice of bread.

Snack

Pretzel sticks, fruit juice

Dinner

Bacon burgers, rolls, baked beans, ketchup, mustard, pickles, tomato slices, hot potato salad, watermelon, fruit punch or iced tea.

Baked Beans

One 15 ounce can baked beans (vegetarian or with pork)
1 Tbs molasses

Mix beans and molasses. Heat in saucepan and serve. Or, place in baking dish, and bake in preheated 350° F. oven for 30 minutes. (Baking will produce a crust.) Serves four.

Idea for leftovers: Use any leftover bacon, from the bacon burgers crumbled up, on the leftover baked beans, or as a topping for salads or for scrambled eggs.

Bacon burgers

1 pound ground chuck
1/2 pound bacon
onion slices
tomato slices
condiments (mustard, mayonnaise, pickles, catsup)
hamburger rolls

Fry bacon in skillet. While bacon is cooking, form ground chuck into four patties. When bacon is done, remove and set aside. Cook hamburgers in bacon fat. Arrange on hamburger buns, top each burger with two slices of bacon, and serve. Serves four.

Hot potato salad

1 pound potatoes, washed (peeling optional)
1/2 medium onion
olive oil
1 clove garlic, minced or 1/2 tsp. garlic powder
1/2 tsp ground oregano

Boil potatoes until tender and cut into bite size pieces. Toss with olive oil, garlic, and oregano and serve while still warm. Serves four.

Sunday, Week Three

Breakfast

Hot cereal, toast, orange slices, fruit juice, coffee or tea

Lunch

Egg salad sandwiches, pears, cookies, milk or iced tea.

Egg salad sandwiches

For each sandwich, you will need

one hard cooked egg
two slices bread
1/8 cup chopped celery
1/8 cup chopped onion
about 1 Tbs. mayonnaise (or more if you wish)

Shell and chop the hard cooked egg in a bowl. Add chopped celery, chopped onion, and mayonnaise. Mix well. Spread on one slice bread. Top with the other slice bread. Slice in half diagonally, if you wish, and serve.

Optional: 1 slice lettuce, placed on egg salad after you have spread it on the bottom slice of bread.

Snack

Ice cream, cola drink, or coffee

Hors d'ouevre

Stuffed cherry tomatoes

1 pint cherry tomatoes
stuffing (recipes below)

Wash the cherry tomatoes, removing green stems. If you wish, shave a really small piece off the bottom to help the cherry tomato sit up straight. With a paring knife or potato peeler, core the cherry tomatoes and remove the insides, taking care not to pierce the walls of the tomatoes. Stuff with blue cheese or cottage cheese stuffings (recipes follow). Insert stuffing into each tomato and refrigerate for about one hour. Makes 24 to 32 hors d'ouevres.

Blue cheese stuffing

1/4 cup crumbled blue cheese
one 3 ounce package cream cheese
small amount milk, as needed
1/4 medium onion, minced fine

Mix crumbled blue cheese, softened cream cheese, and a little milk, if the mixture is too stiff, with the onion. Stuff into the tomatoes.

Variation: substitute crab meat for the blue cheese.

Cottage cheese and onion stuffing

3 scallions, and sliced very finely (or use minced onion)
1/2 cup cottage cheese
dash Worcestershire sauce, dash hot sauce or dash cayenne pepper

Mix ingredients and stuff the tomatoes.

Dinner

Bow tie pasta with salmon, scallions and tomato, rolls, green salad, white wine, coffee or tea.

Bow tie pasta with scallions, salmon and tomato

1/2 pound bow tie pasta
3 or 4 green onions (scallions) sliced crosswise
1 seven ounce can salmon (or use leftover cooked salmon, or buy 1 salmon filet, poach it, and flake into pasta)
1 medium tomato, chopped
Italian seasoning (marjoram, oregano, thyme, basil)
dash garlic powder (optional)
olive oil
salt and pepper

Prepare water for pasta; use about six quarts lightly salted water; bring to a boil and add pasta, stirring frequently, until pasta is cooked to *al dente*, or if you prefer, to slightly more well done than *al dente*. While the water is coming to a boil, chop the scallions and place in a bowl.

Flake the salmon into the bowl and chop the tomato, adding it to the salmon and onion mixture. Season with the Italian seasoning and the garlic, if desired. When the pasta is cooked, drain and return to cooking pot. Add the salmon, scallion and tomato mixture and the olive oil and toss well. Serve immediately. Serves four. This dish may also be made with other types of pasta, such as elbow macaroni or sea shells. Serves four.

Prepare a green salad with your choice of dressing, and serve rolls and butter and a chilled white wine, perhaps a sauvignon blanc, with the meal.

Chapter Eight

Stocking up for Week Four

BACK TO the supermarket, but first, check your pantry or larder and the menus for Week Four. Pick up the items you have used up during the past week and will need again, as well as any new items you plan to use in Week Four. Check the always theres™ and replace those always theres™ that have been consumed.

Remember that items can always be substituted, with good results. For example, a dinner menu might call for veal chops, rice, and brussels sprouts. You could just as easily prepare the veal chops and serve them with sweet potatoes and zuccini. Or serve pork chops instead of the veal chops. That's one of the reasons you have a stock of always theres™.

Dairy Products

Cream cheese

Cheddar cheese, grated, eight ounces

Cottage cheese, fifteen or sixteen ounces. Ricotta can be substituted for cottage cheese. If you are watching your calorie intake, low-fat or no-fat cottage cheese is available in many supermarkets.

Eggs: one dozen (or more, if you eat lots of eggs)

Swiss cheese: 1/2 to 1 pound (depends on how many you are serving)

Meat and Fish

Bacon: check bacon supply and buy a pound of sliced bacon, if you are out.

Beef roast, about 2 and 1/2 pounds: if more than four people are to be served, add about 1/2 pound per person.

Hamburger, or a hamburger and veal mixture: one pound

Chicken, one, cut up

Chicken livers: eight ounces (if you plan to use chicken livers in the mini-mixed grill)

Italian sausage: one pound, in links. You can use either sweet, hot, or Italian sausage (herbs added)

Pork chops: one pound

Steaks: four, about 2 to four ounces each (if you plan to use small steaks in the mini-mixed grill). You can purchase a single steak and cut it into desired portions.

Turkey: 1 frozen, between 10 to 14 pounds (to serve 6 to 8); leftovers can be used in other recipes.

Whitefish: one pound

Produce

Asparagus, 1/4 pound per person. If you have more than you need, cook all of it, and save it to serve with scrambled eggs.

Avocados: one or two. This fruit is good in salads, peeled, sliced and left uncooked. It can be mashed and mixed with lime juice and hot sauce for guacamole dip and served with tortilla chips.

Bananas: three or four

Broccoli: if you plan on using fresh broccoli

Celery: one stalk

Cranberries: if you're planning to make cranberry sauce from scratch. (If not, buy canned cranberry sauce.)

Grapefruit: one; or two oranges.

Grapes: one bunch of seedless, red or green (about one pound). These are great for snacks.

Lemons: one or two

Lettuce: one head. Iceberg, romaine, or Boston are all okay.

Mushrooms: 1/4 pound per person.

Nectarines: plums, or peaches. If the store has some of these fruits, and they look attractive, try some. You might also try cherries in season. If you can't find fresh, try these fruits canned.

Oranges: three to six medium oranges. Some for eating and some for salad.

Onions: four to six medium onions, or more, if you find that onions seem to be used up pretty rapidly.

Pears: one per person.

Peppers: red and green. Get about two medium bell peppers per person, in about a two-to-one ratio of red to green.

Potatoes: five pounds. Russet or redskins are good.

Spinach: one pound of fresh spinach, for spinach salad. (In salads, only fresh spinach will do, although fresh or frozen spinach can be used in cooked or baked dishes.)

Strawberries: one pint to one pound, depending on how much fruit you eat.

Tomatoes: one pound

Frozen (or fresh) products

Check your inventory. How are the frozen vegetables holding out? Time to replenish any of them? If so, perhaps you need:

Frozen bagels: if you don't have fresh bagels available where you live, buy some frozen bagels. They keep well and a regular bagel contains no fat.

Frozen broccoli, if you don't plan to use fresh

Frozen green beans

Frozen corn

Frozen fruit juice. Buy fresh or canned fruit juice if you prefer.

Frozen peas

Frozen spinach, chopped

Staples

Baking mix, pepper, rice, salt, sugar, bullion cubes, bread crumbs. Chances are, you have enough of these items, but you may find you are using some of them faster than you had expected to. For example, frequent baking can cause you to go through lots of flour, baking mix and sugar. That's why it is a good idea to check on what you have in the household each week.

Parmesan cheese, grated: buy some of this fresh cheese is sold, and have them grate it for you. Or buy some in the cardboard canister. The fresh cheese tastes better, but either is good.

Popover mix: you'll be using it with the roast beef.

Pretzels: pick some up if you enjoy them.

Canned foods

Cranberry sauce, one 15 or 16-ounce can.

Evaporated milk, one 6 ounce can.

Fruit juice or vegetable juice. Vegetable juice is often sold under the label "vegetable juice cocktail."

Grape jelly, one eight to ten ounce jar.

Mustard, one six-ounce jar.

Peanut butter, one jar.

Check to see if you need to replenish canned soups, applesauce, canned potatoes, or other canned items.

Dried foods

As you've noticed by now, a lot of dried foods are also staples.

Matzoh cake meal, one-half pound to one pound box. Matzoh cake meal is available in many large supermarkets.

Oatmeal. Check your supply of oatmeal and pick some up. This cereal comes in a number of forms, including "quick," that takes about five minutes to cook, or "instant," that takes about one to two minutes to prepare.

Granola cereal, small box.

Rice, one box. Check to make certain your rice supply is adequate, and if not, get some more.

Baked goods

Bagels, fresh or frozen. Fresh is generally considered better.

English muffins. These come in packages of four, six, or twelve. Choose the size that is right for you.

Raisin bread, one loaf (or, if you already have some in your freezer, use some of that).

Stuffing mix. Herb or chicken flavor is good. About eight ounces.

White bread. Any left from last week? If not, pick some up.

Wines and spirits (optional)

Beer, one six pack

White wine, 4/5 liter.

Chapter Nine

Menus and Recipes for Week Four

THE RECIPES are getting a little more complex, and a lot more delicious and fun. By now, you've had successes and failures, but you're on a solid success track. Congratulations! Keep going!

Monday

Breakfast: Bacon and parsley scrambled eggs on English muffin halves, juice, coffee or tea.

Lunch: Cream cheese and banana sandwiches on raisin bread, grapefruit sections or orange slices, iced tea.

Snack: Parmesan popcorn, apple

Dinner: Pork chops with mustard sauce, rice, spinach, orange, lemon and onion salad, red wine or iced tea, pound cake and fresh blueberries.

Tuesday

Breakfast: Raisin bread French toast, fruit, coffee or tea.

Lunch: Peanut butter and bacon sandwiches on white toast, mineral water, apple.

Snack: Fruit juice, pretzels

Dinner: Grilled or pan fried whitefish, savory baked onions, green beans, baked potatoes, white wine, fresh grapes.

Wednesday

Breakfast: Bagels and cream cheese, juice, coffee or tea.

Lunch: Swiss cheese and lettuce sandwiches, cranberry sauce, sparkling water, Ceil's Passover cookies.

Snack: Celery sticks stuffed with cottage cheese; fruit or vegetable juice.

Dinner: Roast beef and gravy, oven roasted potatoes, oven roasted onions and carrots. Garbanzo bean and red bell pepper salad. Red wine or mineral water. Peach halves with liqueur.

Thursday

Breakfast: Mini-mixed grill: bacon, sausage, tomato slices, sauteed mushrooms, toast triangles, sauteed onions, juice, coffee, tea.

Lunch: Onion gratinee, bread or rolls, green salad, iced tea.

Snack: Pear, hot tea

Dinner: Shepherd's pie, onion and beet salad, gelatin dessert with fruit.

Friday

Breakfast: Oatmeal with strawberries or blueberries, toast with butter or jelly, coffee or tea.

Lunch: Spinach, mushroom and bacon salad, with hard cooked eggs and tomatoes or avocados, rolls, butter, white wine or lemonade.

Snack: Cookies, milk. Alternative: grapes.

Dinner: Fettuccine Alfredo, asparagus salad, hard rolls, Tira Misu II or cheese and fruit.

Saturday

Breakfast: Cold cereal, toast, butter and jelly, applesauce or sliced apples,

Lunch: Fast turkey pie, apple sauce, bread and butter, iced coffee, sorbet or sherbet.

Snack: Granola mix, fruit juice

Dinner: Italian sausage, peppers and onions, pan fried potatoes with oregano, pears, iced tea.

Sunday

Breakfast: Frozen waffles with syrup and butter, bacon, fruit or juice, coffee or tea.

Lunch: Swedish meat balls in gravy, noodles, broccoli, orange and strawberry salad, milk, cookies

Snack: Ice or ice cream on a stick or in a dish.

Hors d'ouevre: Cheddar or Swiss cheese on crackers.

Dinner: Zippy chicken, green bean bake, rice, apple sauce, rolls, pound cake with strawberry sauce.

Monday, Week Four

Breakfast

Bacon and parsley scrambled eggs on English muffin halves, toast or roll, fruit or juice, coffee or tea.

Parsley scrambled eggs

Use scrambled egg recipe from Wednesday, Week One (page 75), and add 1 tsp. of chopped fresh parsley per egg.

Bacon

Use bacon recipe from Wednesday, Week One (page 71).

Lunch

Cream cheese and banana sandwiches on raisin bread, grapefruit sections or orange slices, cookies, iced tea.

Cream cheese and banana sandwiches on raisin bread

For each sandwich, you will need:

1 ounce cream cheese, softened
1/2 banana, sliced
two slices raisin bread

Thinly spread cream cheese on each slice of bread. Slice banana, and place banana slices on one of the bread slices. Top with the other bread slice.

Snack

Parmesan popcorn, apple.

Dinner

Pork chops with mustard sauce, rice, spinach salad with orange, lemon and onion slices, red wine or iced tea, pound cake, fresh strawberries.

Pork chops

The menu for Thursday Week One, calls for a pork chop and rice casserole. Here's another way to serve pork with rice.

4 pork chops (about one pound)
small amount oil for frying
pinch ground sage

Heat oil in skillet over medium heat. Fry pork chops until brown on one side. Sprinkle uncooked side with sage and turn over. Sprinkle other side with sage and continue cooking until cooked through. Pork should be cooked well done. (Serves four.)

Mustard sauce

4 Tbs. prepared mustard
2 Tbs olive oil or salad oil
pinch ground sage
pinch black pepper

Mix ingredients well and serve over pork chops.

Spinach with curry (or nutmeg)

1 ten ounce box frozen chopped spinach.
1/2 Tsp curry powder

Place a small amount of water in a saucepan, put the spinach inside, and heat over low to medium flame, until the spinach has thawed and is cooked. Sprinkle with curry powder and toss, then serve.

Variation: if you do not enjoy curry, try nutmeg instead.

Rice

Use 1/4 cup uncooked rice per person. Because rice is so useful in leftovers, you may want to cook extra. Serves four.

1 cup uncooked rice.
1 Tbs. oil or butter
2 cups water
1/8 tsp. salt (optional)

Place uncooked rice in saucepan. Pour oil over rice and stir until each grain is coated with thin film of oil. Pour in water and add the salt. Bring to a boil, then turn heat down to lowest setting and cook for about twenty minutes, or until all water has been absorbed into the rice and rice is done. Fluff with fork and serve.

Variation: use one of the potato recipes in this book in place of the rice.

Tuesday, Week Four

Breakfast

Raisin bread French toast, fruit, coffee or tea.

Raisin bread French toast

For each serving:
2 slices white or whole wheat raisin bread
1 egg
splash of milk
oil for cooking
sugar or syrup
cinnamon (optional)

Heat oil in skillet over medium flame. Beat egg(s) and milk with a fork. Place in shallow bowl. Dip each side of a bread slice in egg mixture and place in hot skillet. Brown on one side, then the other. Serve with syrup, or powdered sugar and cinnamon.

Lunch

Peanut butter and bacon sandwiches on white toast, mineral water, apple.

Peanut butter and bacon sandwiches

For each sandwich, you will need:

two slices white toast
peanut butter, spread thinly on each slice of toast
two or three strips cooked bacon.

Toast the bread, and spread peanut butter on the upper face of each slice. Add cooked bacon to one slice, then top with the other slice. Cut into halves. Serve with mineral water, with an apple for dessert.

Variations: bread and peanut butter are a sure-fire combination. You can add thinly sliced raw onions to the peanut butter and bacon sandwich, or use peanut butter and apple, or peanut butter and sliced cheddar cheese as variations instead of bacon.

Snack

Fruit juice, pretzels.

Dinner

Grilled or pan fried whitefish, savory baked onions, green beans, baked potatoes, white wine, fresh grapes.

Grilled or pan fried whitefish

If you're planning to grill the whitefish, prepare the grill and light the fire. If you're planning to pan fry the whitefish, place some oil in a skillet or cast iron frying pan and turn the heat to low.

For each serving, you will need:

1 whitefish filet (use whitefish, a fish that is found in the Great Lakes, or any other lake or ocean white-fleshed fish, such as sole or flounder. Have your butcher or fish merchant clean the fish.)
parsley for garnish
lemon slices for garnish

Unwrap the whitefish and rinse in cold water. Pat dry with paper towels. Place the whitefish on the grill or in the frying pan and cook until browned on that side. Turn the filet over and cook until cooked through. Cooked fish loses the translucent appearance of raw fish and is opaque.

Heads up. Fish cooks quite quickly. Don't leave the stove or grill area. It is likely the fish will be cooked through in seven or eight minutes, or possibly less. Cooking time depends upon the thickness of the fish.

Idea for leftovers: saute some onion and chop the cooked whitefish into the onion until warm. Break one egg per person into the cooked onion and warmed whitefish and scramble. Serve with toast.

Green beans

Use one of the green beans recipes from Monday, Week One (p. 85); or buy fresh green beans, and wash, remove ends and boil in just enough water to cover until they reach the desired degree of doneness.

Tip: Pressed for time? use canned green beans or microwave frozen green beans as in recipe for Monday, Week One, (p. 85).

Baked potatoes

Use one of the recipes from Monday, Week One (page 64).

Savory baked onions

For each person, you will need

1/2 medium onion
1 Tbs. bread crumbs
1/8 tsp. minced garlic or garlic powder or to taste
chopped parsley to taste
1/4 tsp sherry or wine (optional)
ground oregano to taste (optional)
small amount of oil.

Preheat oven to 350°F. Cut onion in half. Set with cut side facing up. Mix bread crumbs, garlic, parsley, and oregano and cover top of onion. Drizzle about 1/2 tsp (or an amount to your taste) of oil, preferably olive oil, onto the bread crumb mixture, and about 1/4 tsp sherry if you wish.

Broil or bake in oven at 350°f., for about 20 minutes or until topping is brown.

Idea for leftovers: use any leftover onion in a tossed salad or as garnish or sliced with bagels and cream cheese.

Wednesday, Week Four

Breakfast

Bagels and cream cheese, juice, coffee or tea.

Bagels

Bagels are a bread product that has been boiled, then baked. Bagels are available fresh or frozen. Spread sliced bagels with cream cheese. They can be split and toasted first, if you desire.

Optional "go well together" items with bagels are:

lox (salted sliced smoked salmon)
tomato slices
onion slices or chopped onion
capers
chopped parsley

Variation: if you prefer, use English muffins or toast instead of bagels.

Lunch

Swiss cheese and lettuce sandwiches, cranberry sauce, sparkling water, cookies.

Swiss cheese and lettuce sandwiches

For each sandwich, you will need:

2 slices bread
one or two slices Swiss cheese
one or two leaves lettuce
mayonnaise or mustard

Spread sandwich spread on two slices of bread. Top one slice with Swiss cheese, then lettuce. Cover with second slice. Repeat for each person to be served.

Cranberry sauce

Cranberry sauce isn't just for turkey. It is surprisingly good with many foods. Use a can of whole or jellied cranberry sauce, or make your own. If you are making cranberry sauce from scratch, buy a one pound bag of fresh cranberries and do the following:

Scratch cranberry sauce

1 pound fresh cranberries, washed
1/2 cup to 1 cup sugar
1 cup water.

Boil cranberries, sugar and water together until cranberries have burst; stir, cool and serve.

Ceil's Passover cookies

These cookies are good all year round, and they can be made the night before.

1 cup (2 sticks) butter
3/4 cup sugar
1/2 tsp. salt
1 tsp. vanilla
two eggs, separated
1 cup matzoh cake meal
and 1/2 cup chopped nuts
jam or preserves for centers

Cream butter, sugar, vanilla and salt until light and fluffy. Beat egg yolks well and add to butter mixture. Blend in matzoh cake meal with a spatula (more meal may be needed). Chill dough in ice box for one hour.

When you remove the dough from the refrigerator, preheat the oven to 350° F. Form into 1 inch balls. Beat the egg whites and dip the balls into the beaten egg whites. Roll balls in chipped nuts until they are covered with nuts. Flatten the balls into cookies and place on a lightly greased cookie sheet. Press down the centers. Bake for 15 minutes. Remove from the oven and press down the centers again.

Cool cookies and fill the centers with jam.

Snack

Celery sticks stuffed with cottage cheese; and vegetable or fruit juice.

Dinner

Roast beef and gravy, oven roasted potatoes, oven roasted onions and carrots. Garbanzo bean and red pepper salad. Red wine or mineral water. Peach halves with liqueur (optional).

Roast beef with oven roasted onions, potatoes and carrots

This recipe serves four persons, with some leftovers.

one boneless rolled beef roast, about 3 to 3 and 1/2 pounds
two large or three medium potatoes, washed but not peeled (peel them if you wish, but it's just extra work and the skins are good for you)
two medium or one large onion, peeled
three carrots, washed (peeling optional) and cut into two inch pieces.
small amount olive oil

Preheat oven to 400°F. Prepare vegetables and cut into pieces. Place the olive oil in a large bowl and put all of the vegetables into the bowl. Toss so that each piece is very lightly coated with olive oil. Unwrap the beef and pat dry with paper towels. Place the roast beef in a roasting pan and place the vegetables around it.

Place the roasting pan into the oven and roast for 1/2 hour at 400°F. Then reduce heat to 350°F. Cook about 20 minutes per pound for rare, and 25 minutes per pound for medium but at least for one hour. Your butcher may have wrapped all or a portion of the beef roast with fat (white, as opposed to the red of the meat). If you wish, about halfway through the process place some red wine, or beef broth, or both (perhaps a total of one and one-half cups) in the bottom of the roasting pan. The results are fabulous.

Brown Gravy

Now it can be told. Good gravy is a mixture of pan drippings, which often include fat, scraped bits from the bottom of the pan, flour, and water. If additional fat is needed, a small amount of butter can be added. Commercial gravies are quite good, as well. Note that canned gravies often include high amounts of salt.

If you are making the gravy from scratch, you should do the following:

Remove the roast and vegetables and let them "rest" about ten minutes. Slice a small piece out of the middle of the roast to test for doneness. If the roast needs more time in the oven, return to oven. If not, make the gravy.

1. Pour all of the liquids from the bottom of the pan into a skillet. If you wish, spoon off most of the fat or pour it off.

2. Light burner under the skillet. Scrape the browned bits of the bottom of the roasting pan. Add them to the liquids in the skillet.

3. Add a small amount of flour (about 1/2 teaspoon) to the sauces in the skillet. Stir constantly until the flour has cooked.

Now here's the secret--the flour has to *cook*--so make sure the gravy in the skillet is heated to bubbling for a couple of minutes. That temperature will cook the flour. If the gravy is too thin, gradually add more flour, a little at a time until the gravy reaches the desired thickness. The gravy will be getting thicker also, from the evaporation of some of the liquids. Stir the gravy constantly. Serve in a pitcher or gravy boat with the roast.

4. Slice the roast and serve with the gravy.

Ideas for leftovers--Roast beef sandwiches, roast beef hash (cut up roast beef and cut up potatoes, sauteed in a frying pan with some onions), cold sliced roast beef with tomatoes, hard-cooked eggs, romaine lettuce, green onions, and pickled beets--the list is endless.

Fast gravy

Open a can or jar of commercial prepared beef gravy about five minutes before you remove the roast from the oven. Heat over low temperature, stirring occasionally and serve with the roast and vegetables. You will discover it isn't bad at all.

Garbanzo bean and sweet red bell pepper salad

This colorful salad can be served cold, at room temperature, or warm. If you like a slightly more piquant taste, add 1 tsp. balsalmic vinegar.

1 fifteen ounce can garbanzo beans (also known as chick peas or chi-chi beans) rinsed and drained
2 sweet red bell peppers, washed, cored, seeded and cut up
1/4 cup chopped green onions (other onion can be substituted)
2 to 3 Tbs. olive oil
black pepper
fresh parsley, chopped (optional)

Combine beans, red pepper and green onions. Toss with oil. Add pepper, parsley, vinegar if desired, and toss again. This salad is very brightly colored, and adds a lot of visual impact to a plate. Tastes good, too.

Peach halves with liqueur

4 peach halves (use fresh or canned).
4 Tbs. liqueur, such as creme de menthe, peach schnapps or Drambuie. Raspberry syrup may be substituted for the liqueur.

Refrigerate peach halves and top with liqueur or syrup before serving.

Variation: use ice cream instead of liqueur. Or use them both.

Thursday, Week Four

Breakfast

This breakfast is for special occasions or those days when you need a really hearty breakfast.

Mini-mixed grill. Bacon, sausage, tomato slices or tomatoes Provencal, sauteed mushrooms on toast points, sauteed onions, fruit juice, coffee or tea.

Toast points

Toast points is another name for a slice of toast cut diagonally twice, so that each slice yields four triangle shaped pieces. Use sliced bread, about 2 slices per person. Toast the bread and do not butter. Cut each slice diagonally, then diagonally again, to make four toast triangles from each slice of bread.

Sauteed mushrooms

eight ounces to one pound of mushrooms (more if you really like mushrooms, less if you don't)
2 Tbs olive oil
1 Tbs butter
small amount red or white wine

Clean mushrooms with damp paper towel, removing any specks of dirt. Melt butter in skillet over low flame or heat and when butter has melted, add the olive oil, then the mushrooms. Stir frequently. The mushrooms will give up a good deal of liquid. After about four or five minutes, when each mushroom has been coated with the oil and butter mixture, add the wine and simmer for about ten minutes, or until the mushrooms are done. The mushrooms may be sauteed ahead of time, even the night before, and warmed up just before adding to the mixed grill. If they are made ahead of time, be sure to refrigerate overnight. Arrange toast points on each plate and serve mushrooms and mini-mixed grill over the toast points.

Mini-mixed grill

4 slices bacon
4 links breakfast sausage
8 ounces chicken livers or 4 small steaks (optional)
2 medium tomatoes
bread for toasting (four to eight slices)
chicken stock for chicken livers

Wash and slice tomatoes and set aside. Or, if you wish, prepare the tomatoes Provencal.

Tomatoes Provencal

2 medium tomatoes
1/4 cup regular or seasoned bread crumbs (seasoned preferred)
small amount olive oil
Parmesan cheese
parsley

Preheat oven to 350° F. Cut tomatoes in half. Remove small piece from bottom and sit tomatoes upright. Place bread crumbs on top of each tomato, top with small amount Parmesan cheese, chopped parsley and a drop or two of olive oil. Bake for 30 minutes or until done.

Cook bacon and sausage. For sausage, place a small amount of water (about 1/4 cup) in a skillet and gently simmer the sausage for about ten minutes. Pierce the sausage with a fork to permit juices to escape. The water will evaporate, and the sausage will brown. The sausage can also be cooked by placing it into the bacon pan after you have prepared the bacon and drained off most of the fat.

After cooking the sausage and bacon, pan fry or grill the steaks or, if you are using the chicken livers, cook them. Place bacon, sausage, and steaks on a platter and cover with aluminum foil. Then cook the chicken livers.

Chicken livers

8 ounces chicken livers
2 cups chicken stock
1/2 onion, chopped

Place about 1/2 cup stock in a skillet and heat the onions for about five minutes. While the onion is cooking, wash and remove the white fatty parts and any membrane from the chicken livers. Place the livers in the hot stock with the onions and cook, over medium heat adding more stock if needed. Gradually let stock diminish until it is almost all gone and livers are cooked (they will turn from dark red to light brown).

If you're serving steaks, see the recipe for steaks in Chapter Three, Saturday, Week One.

Assemble bacon, sausage, steaks or chicken livers, and mushrooms on toast triangles along with tomatoes Provencal on plate. Serves four.

Lunch

Onion gratinee, bread or rolls, green salad, iced tea, fruit.

Onion gratinee

one very large large cooking onion, or two medium onions
four eggs
1 cup Parmesan cheese
1/2 cup pitted black olives, chopped
butter or olive oil (or both) for sauteing

Preheat oven to 350° F. Peel onion and slice in half from top to bottom. Slice crosswise and separate into half rings. In skillet, melt butter and saute onions over medium heat, until translucent and soft. Add olives, and saute about one minute. Beat eggs lightly and add Parmesan cheese. Place in oven for about 20 minutes or until browned and puffed up. Serve immediately. Serves four

Tossed green salad

Use tossed green salad recipe from Tuesday, Week One, or make up your own recipe. By now you know that any salad greens, washed and drained will make a pretty good salad when paired with a good dressing. For example, a little oil, vinegar and some pear and blue cheese slices are a fabulous dressing combination.

Snack

Fresh pear, plum, or nectarine and some hot herbal or regular tea.

Dinner

Shepherd's pie, onion and beet salad, gelatin dessert with fruit.

Shepherd's pie

Preheat oven to 350° F. Shepherd's pie is stew (recipe follows), covered with mashed potatoes, and baked in the oven until the potatoes have been browned. This is a dish that comes from the old Celtic traditions. It can be made with leftover beef (for example, the leftover beef from Wednesday's dinner) or from lamb and from leftover mashed potatoes. It can be made quickly with canned beef stew and instant mashed potatoes. Or you can make mashed potatoes and beef or lamb stew from scratch and combine the two into an excellent version of this dish.

Beef stew (from scratch)

For the stew, you will need:

1 pound stewing beef (or lamb), cut up.
2 or 3 carrots, washed, peeled and cut up
2 medium onions, peeled and cut up
1 celery rib, washed, trimmed and cut up
1 bay leaf
1 eight ounce jar brown gravy or make your own
1 can condensed cream of tomato soup, undiluted
1 cup water
1/4 cup salad oil or olive oil or shortening

Optional step:

In a skillet, brown the beef in the oil or shortening; add the onions and brown them. Strictly speaking, this step is not necessary since the brown gravy and tomato soup will give the beef a good color.

If you are using uncooked carrots, onions, and celery, cut them up and place them in a large bowl with some oil. Toss to lightly coat each piece with the oil. Place them in a baking dish with the beef, the bay leaf, the soup, water, and pepper to taste. The recipe does not need salt as there is a good deal of salt in the soup and gravy. Add the brown gravy and mix well. Cook at 350° F. for one hour. Remove from oven, cover with mashed potatoes, and cook for another 15 to 20 minutes. Serves six.

If you are using canned beef stew, or leftover cooked stew, all you have to do is warm it up. In that case, remove it from the oven after 15 minutes and cover with the mashed potatoes.

Mashed potatoes

4 medium potatoes, washed, peeled, and cut up into chunks
milk, 1/4 cup to 1/2 cup
butter, to taste

Mashed potatoes are best made from russet (Idaho, Long Island, or Maine) potatoes; or from Yukon Gold potatoes, although redskins can also be used. Place the potatoes in a covered pot and cover them with water, to a level of about one inch over the potatoes. Bring water to boil, and cook until a fork pierces them easily. Drain the potatoes, and mash them, adding milk and butter as desired. Cover the stew with the potatoes.

Brown gravy

Use leftover brown gravy from Wednesday dinner, this week, (p. 179), make some from scratch using the recipe from Wednesday dinner, or open a can or jar of brown gravy and use that.

Variation: this dish can be made with a biscuit crust instead of a mashed potato crust. Just use the biscuit recipe from Friday, Week One, and drop the biscuits over the stew in spoonfuls to cover.

Onion and beet salad

1 can sliced beets
onion slices
vinegar
oil
salt and pepper

Drain beets. Take 1 Tbs. beet liquid and mix with 3 Tbs. oil and 2 Tbs. vinegar. Mix beets with onion slices. Toss with dressing. Season with salt and pepper.

Variation--use orange slices in addition to or instead of onions.

Gelatin dessert with fruit

1 box gelatin dessert mix
1 eight ounce can sliced peaches, or other such canned or fresh fruit, such as plums, pears, fruit cocktail.

Follow package directions (this calls for dissolving the gelatin powder by pouring hot water into it), and place fruit in liquid gelatin dessert. Chill about two hours and serve. Gelatin dessert is really easy to prepare. Just empty the package into a bowl, add boiling water, and let cool, then refrigerate. The packages suggest faster ways of preparing this dessert as well.

Prepared or "store-bought" gelatin

Many stores sell individual packages of prepared gelatin or pudding desserts. Great idea when you're in a hurry, but like many convenience foods, more costly than the kind you mix yourself.

Heads up: gelatin dessert won't set or "jell" if it is made with pineapple or kiwi fruit. They contain an enzyme that prevents the gelatin from "setting up."

Friday, Week Four

Breakfast

Oatmeal with strawberries or blueberries, toast with butter or jelly, coffee or tea.

Oatmeal

1 portion oatmeal per serving (see package directions)
hot water as necessary (see package directions)

Prepare oatmeal according to package directions. There are several kinds of oatmeal available, ranging from old fashioned, which cook in ten minutes, to instant (about one minute).

Strawberries

Wash and hull the strawberries, or wash the blueberries, add to cereal and serve.

Lunch

Spinach salad, with bacon and mushrooms, hard cooked eggs, and tomato or avocado slices.

Spinach, bacon and mushroom salad

1 pound spinach, washed, drained, and dried in towel or spun dry in salad spinner
4 hard boiled eggs, peeled and sliced
1/2 pound bacon, cooked and crumbled
1/2 pound fresh mushrooms, wiped clean, trimmed if necessary, and sliced
1 large tomato, or two medium tomatoes, sliced
oil and vinegar dressing

Wash the spinach, and drain it. To dry in a towel, spread a dish towel on a clean surface and roll the spinach up in the towel until dry. Repeat if necessary until all the spinach has been dried. Or spin in a salad spinner, available at cooking equipment stores. Arrange on four plates. Crumble bacon onto spinach and add mushrooms. Slice eggs and arrange on plates, along with tomato slices. Drizzle with oil and vinegar dressing and serve with rolls.

Variation: substitute avocado slices for tomato slices.

Snack

Cookies and milk.

Alternative snack: fresh grapes.

Have some of your favorite cookies with a glass of milk. Or have some green or red seedless grapes.

Dinner

Fettucine Alfredo, asparagus salad, hard rolls, Tira Misu II or cheese and fruit.

Fettucine Alfredo

1 pound fettucine or linguine pasta.
1 stick butter
1/c cup (4 ounces) heavy cream
Parmesan or Romano cheese to taste
chopped fresh parsley, to taste (optional)

Bring pasta to a boil and cook until done, al dente (slightly resistant to the tooth) style. Meanwhile, cut the stick of butter into about 16 pieces, and separate. Chop the parsley, and have the cream ready. When the pasta is ready, drain it quickly and return it to the pot, which you have taken off the heat. Working quickly, add the butter pieces, then the cream, and mix well. The butter will melt, mix with the cream, and cook in the hot pasta. Add the Parmesan cheese and serve immediately. Garnish with fresh chopped parsley.

Saturday, Week Four

Breakfast

Cold cereal, toast and butter or jelly, juice, coffee or tea, applesauce or baked or sliced apples.

If you're planning to serve baked apples, use the baked apple recipe from Tuesday, Week One (page 68).

Lunch

Fast turkey pie, broiled tomatoes, green peas, mineral water, plums or pears.

Fast turkey "pie"

This is a crustless pie that can be prepared in a pie plate.

1 six or seven ounce package stuffing mix
cup chopped cooked turkey or chicken (or 1 seven ounce can of chicken)
1 cup shredded Swiss cheese
1 small onion, chopped
1 small can evaporated (not condensed) milk
1/8 teaspoon black pepper (or white pepper)
chopped parsley, to taste

Preheat oven to 400° F. Prepare the stuffing according to package directions, and press the stuffing into a 9" pie plate. Bake for ten minutes. Mix chicken, Swiss cheese, onion, and place in hot pie crust. In a bowl, beat together eggs, milk and pepper. Pour egg mixture over chicken mixture. Reduce oven temperature to 350° F., and bake 30 to 35 minutes until center is set. Let stand ten minutes. Garnish with parsley or with orange wedges or tomato wedges

Variation: this recipe works well with tuna fish instead of poultry. Use one regular sized can (about 6.5 to 7 ounces) of tuna fish.

Broiled tomatoes

For each person, you will need:

1/2 tomato
small amount of butter
1/4 tsp. sugar (optional)
chopped parsley (optional)

Turn on oven broiler to preheat. Place tomato halves on a tray, cut sides up, and place a small pat of butter on each tomato half. Sprinkle with the sugar. Broil for a few moments until butter has melted. Sprinkle with the parsley.

Green peas

Use canned green peas and warm up in saucepan or microwave; or open a box (10 ounces) or bag (16 ounces) of frozen green peas, shake out the amount you want to serve, and microwave or heat in saucepan.

Tip: microwaves vary in intensity and cooking time. For canned peas, warm up for about two minutes, turn and warm up for another two minutes. For frozen peas, add about 1 tsp. of water to the peas, cover, leaving a small opening for steam to escape, and microwave for three minutes. Rotate 90 degrees, stir the peas, and microwave again for three minutes. The peas should be done.

Variation: add finely chopped onion or sliced mushrooms to the peas.

Snack

Granola mix or granola bar; fruit juice.

Dinner

Italian sausage, peppers and onions; pan fried potatoes; beer, red wine, or cola; avocado, lettuce and orange salad, bread or rolls, ice cream.

Italian sausage, peppers, and onions

One pound Italian sweet link sausage (or 1/2 pound sweet and 1/2 pound hot)
four bell peppers, two red and two green
1 large onion.
eight ounces tomato sauce
bay leaf
olive oil
oregano

Pierce each sausage link with a fork and simmer in a skillet in about 1/8 inch water (barely enough to cover bottom of skillet) over medium heat. Gradually, the juices from the sausage will seep out and the sausages will brown in their own juices as the water evaporates. In a separate skillet, saute the onion and green peppers in some olive oil.

When the sausages have browned, add them to the peppers and onions, and cover with tomato sauce. Simmer, covered, for about twenty minutes, or until the peppers and onions are soft and the sausage has been cooked through. Serve with potatoes and bread or rolls. (Serves four).

Pan fried potatoes

two medium potatoes, washed and sliced thin
oil, if needed

After the sausages have been transferred to the skillet containing the peppers and onions, drain, place the potatoes, into the pan where the sausages have cooked and cook them over medium high heat, so they will be ready when the sausage and peppers are ready. Stir frequently, turning once or twice.

Variation: serve the sausages with rice or pasta instead of potatoes.

Sunday, Week Four

Breakfast

Frozen waffles, bacon, fruit or juice, coffee or tea.

Lunch

Swedish meat balls in gravy, noodles, broccoli, orange and strawberry salad, milk, cookies.

Swedish meat balls

You can find canned Swedish meatballs in gravy in the canned meats section of your super market; and there are frozen versions on the market as well. Or you can make them from scratch.

1 pound ground chuck or mixture of hamburger and ground veal
1 cup bread crumbs
small amount milk or cream
small amount salt and pepper
1 egg, lightly beaten
oil for sauteing
2 cups chicken or beef stock

Mix ingredients well (the egg helps hold the meatballs together) and form balls one inch in diameter. Meanwhile, heat the stock and two cups of water to a simmer. Brown the meatballs in a skillet. As they brown, drop them into the hot stock. Bring liquid to a boil and cook until done, about 20 minutes. Serves six, or makes 40 meatballs for hors d'ouevres.

Sauce for Swedish meatballs

two eight ounce cans brown gravy
one eight-to-ten ounce jar grape jelly (honest!)
one eight ounce can tomato sauce.

Mix ingredients together and simmer until well-blended. This makes a most interesting sauce for the meatballs.

Snack

Sherbet or ice cream on a stick.

Hors d'ouevre

Cheddar cheese crackers.

This great hors d'ouevre is really easy to make and has only three ingredients.

eight ounces butter (two sticks)
1 cup flour
1 cup shredded cheddar cheese

Preheat oven to 350°F.. Mash flour into butter and mix cheddar cheese into flour and butter mixture. Be certain to mix well. Roll out on a floured board, or a table top, or a clean flat surface, dusted with flour, to about 1/4 inch depth. Use a round cookie cutter or juice glass to cut the crackers into rounds. Place on cookie sheet and bake for ten minutes or until crisp.

Dinner

Zippy chicken, green bean bake, rice, applesauce, rolls, coffee or tea, pound cake with strawberry sauce.

Zippy chicken

1 chicken, cut up (you can buy it this way at the super market)
1 medium or large onion, chopped
1 carrot, chopped
1 rib celery, chopped
4 medium potatoes, chopped.
1 cup barbecue sauce
1/4 cup olive oil or salad oil
1 bay leaf
salt and pepper to taste

Preheat oven to 375° F. Wash, chop and cut up vegetables (peeling optional). Place oil in bowl and add vegetables, tossing to lightly coat with oil. Remove vegetables and place in baking pan. Rinse chicken parts in cold water, pat dry with paper towels. Place chicken parts in remaining oil, and toss lightly. Add barbecue sauce and toss again.

Place chicken in pan with vegetables. Pour barbecue sauce over chicken and vegetables. Bake for 90 minutes or until chicken is done, basting occasionally. If dish seems dry, add a bit of water or some chicken stock or broth. (You've got chicken bullion cubes in the "always theres™" part of your pantry, right?) Serves four.

Green bean bake

1 16 ounce bag frozen green beans (or two 16 ounce cans green beans, drained).
1 can sliced water chestnuts, drained
1 can condensed cream of mushroom (or chicken or celery or asparagus or broccoli) soup
1/4 soup can milk
1 small jar pimentos (or 1 can onion rings or fresh red pepper rings or crumbled potato chips) as garnish.

Place green beans and water chestnuts in baking dish and mix together. Blend soup and milk and add to bean mixture, blending well. Place garnish on top; cover (use foil if baking dish doesn't have cover) and bake at 375° F. for about one hour. Remove cover for the last ten minutes or so. This recipe does not require added salt. There is plenty in the condensed soup. Serves eight.

Presentation is everything (continued)

Contrast adds to eye appeal of foods. Consider this. Serve a piece of white fish on a white plate. It is tasty, but somewhat bland. Instead, cook a box of frozen chopped spinach, and spread it out on a serving platter. Put the fish on the bed of spinach, and the presentation is much more effective. Surround the fish with lemon slices or cherry tomatoes, and you wind up with a really great look! No lemon slices? Then alternate the tomatoes with mushroom caps. The same principle applies if your serving *crudites,* the hors d'ouevre composed of raw and room temperature vegetables.

White cauliflower flowerets, black pitted olives, green pepper strips, red radishes, orange carrots, green stuffed olives, celery sticks, carrot sticks, and cucumber rounds each contribute vivid color to a vegetable platter. Placing light against dark, red against green, and so forth really brings out the appeal of the individual vegetables.

Chapter Ten

Stocking up for Week Five

BY NOW, you're running a kitchen with a well-stocked pantry. The "always theres™" are standing by, ready to be used in a regular meal, or to help out in a pinch. The foods that are supposed to be fresh, are fresh, and you have pitched anything that isn't. You are headed into the fifth--and final week this book covers. There are a few special items: a buffet for the Big Game; a turkey dinner; and a cocktail party. The shopping list includes a ham, and a whole turkey or turkey breast. Once again, check the "always theres"™ and supplies of fresh, frozen and canned foods, dairy products and staples, and head for the supermarket.

Supplies

If you do not have a roasting pan, buy a large disposable aluminum roasting pan for the roast turkey; and another for the ham.

Dairy products

What's there from last week? From the week prior to that? Check freshness dates, and discard anything out of date.

Milk, two quarts: (more or less, depending on usage).

Butter or margarine: one pound.

Cheddar or Swiss cheese: A six to eight ounce wedge. Use for snacking, or grate or shred it and add to other dishes, such as scrambled eggs or cauliflower. Also use in the celery, fig and cheddar cheese salad, if using this recipe on Saturday night.

Cream cheese, eight ounces.

Dips: 2 eight ounce packages; or make dips with sour cream and dip mix. One envelope of onion soup mix and sixteen ounces of sour cream can be combined to make onion dip.

Hot pepper cheese, eight ounce bar or wedge.

Mozzarella cheese, two pounds.

Sour cream, one pint. (Buy more to make the dips yourself.)

Low-fat alternative: there are low-fat or fat-free sour creams..

Yogurt, one pint.

Meat and Fish

Check supplies of meat, poultry and fish. By now, you know how frequently, you are using these foods. Fill in your "always theres™" supplies, according to your own patterns of use.

Beef: corned, sliced. Try some sliced corned beef, from the deli counter, in Friday's lunch.

Beef: ground, one pound. If using the barbecued hamburger recipe for Saturday night, buy two pounds.

Chicken: One whole breast, boned; or 1 pound of boneless breasts.

Fish: If using the fish recipe for Saturday night, buy one pound sole or whitefish filets, fresh or frozen (to serve four).

Ham: One pound, sliced fairly thin (from the deli department).

Ham: One whole or half ham, precooked, and possibly pre-sliced. There are many alternatives. See **about ham** on p. 219.

Turkey: One whole turkey, frozen, about 10 to 12 pounds, will serve six to eight people. If you're feeding many people, you'll want a slightly larger turkey. A 14 to 16 pound turkey will feed eight to ten, and a larger turkey, still more. Or, you may wish to buy one frozen turkey breast. These frozen turkey breasts usually run six to seven pounds and feed six to eight. Both whole turkeys and breasts are sold with full cooking instructions.

Salmon: Two filets (about 1 pound); or purchase some canned salmon.

Veal: Four veal chops (about 1 pound).

Produce

Apples: buy some for snacking.

Variation: Try pears, nectarines, plums, or peaches, instead..

Asparagus: One pound of asparagus spears. Asparagus spears also come in canned and frozen versions. Canned asparagus does not require cooking, but is not quite as fresh tasting as fresh.

Bananas: four or five bananas (about one pound).

Bell peppers: Five or six green, red, or yellow bell peppers: four for stuffing, and a couple for cooking and/or snacking. Different colored sweet bell peppers can be substituted for one another. Red peppers have a mellower flavor and more vitamin A.than green. Experiment with different colors in a dish.

Blueberries: one pint blueberries.

Cantaloupe or other melon: Buy one or two cantaloupes.

Carrots: 1 pound carrots

Time-saver: carrots can be purchased washed and peeled.

Cauliflower: One medium head. Look for cauliflower that is fresh and all white.

Celery: 1 stalk celery (a stalk usually contains eight to ten individual ribs).

Cranberries: 1 pound cranberries (usually sold fresh around Thanksgiving, frozen the rest of the year). If not making cranberry sauce from scratch, buy a can of prepared cranberry sauce.

Cucumbers: One or two cucumbers. For salads and snacking.

Dates. These are generally sold dried. Buy about 1/2 pound to 1 pound. Dried dates keep well.

Fruit punch: If you are planning to purchase fruit punch, pick up a quart or two. Some fruit punch is sold in the dairy section; canned fruit punch is sold in the juices section.

Grapefruit: Two grapefruit, for breakfast. (Good alternatives are strawberries, melon, or blueberries.)

Juice: Pick up some fresh, frozen, or canned juice.

Lettuce: One head lettuce of your choice.

Nectarines: A good "stone fruit" for snacking and desserts. Others are plums, peaches, and apricots.

Nuts: One pound walnuts, or 1/2 pound chopped walnuts. (Nuts keep well in freezer). If you don't have a nutcracker, buy the nuts already cracked and shelled.

Onions or scallions: Get several white or yellow onions and 1 bunch scallions or green onions.

Peaches: fresh or canned.

Potatoes: Check your supply, and buy some if needed.

Radishes: 1 bunch radishes. These need to be washed and have the green leaves and stems trimmed off before serving; or buy radishes that have been trimmed and washed.

Spinach: Get some fresh spinach if you plan to make the green salad with orange juice dressing.

Squash or zucchini: Pick up three or four zucchini (green) or summer squash (yellow), about a pound, total. Save one squash for the chicken pasta bake.

Strawberries: One pint to one quart, depending on your fruit consumption.

Tangerines or oranges: Several, for snacking, garnishes or salads.

Tomatoes: Buy several for the different recipes and salads this week.

Frozen or fresh products

Coffee cake: One frozen coffee cake. If you have a good bakery nearby, and you're shopping close to the time you are planning to serve the coffee cake, by all means buy a fresh one.

Green beans: If your larder is empty, get one box or bag frozen green beans. Alternatives are fresh or canned.

Juice: Buy frozen juice if you are not purchasing fresh or canned juice.

Squash: Buy frozen squash if you don't buy fresh.

Spinach: One or two boxes frozen chopped spinach.

Staples

Balsalmic vinegar: Pick up a small bottle. This is a dark, flavorful, expensive vinegar that imparts interesting tastes to salads and other dishes. Use it sparingly.

Bread sticks: If you have used up the bag you bought last week, get one bag bread sticks. These keep quite well in a pantry.

Low -fat and low -salt alternatives: Low fat and low salt bread sticks are available

Coffee and tea: How are your supplies? Pick some up, if needed..

Hollandaise sauce: There are dried Hollandaise mixes to which you add water and butter on the market. When it comes to Hollandaise, fresh is better. If making fresh, check the egg supply.

Stuffing: One bag stuffing mix, enough for a 14 pound turkey

Rice: Check your rice supply.

Dried foods

Dates: Buy some dried dates, if using the fig, celery, and cheddar cheese recipe (Saturday night).

Pancake mix: Buy one box pancake mix or baking mix, if needed.

Pasta: Check the pasta supply and pick some up if necessary.

Potato or other chips: If you are a chip eater, or are planning on making salsa, get a bag or two of these. Use in Tuesday's snack, and get more to serve at the Big Game buffet.

Pudding: Get some vanilla pudding mix, instant or cooked type; or buy canned pudding that is ready to eat.

Tomatoes, sun dried: One package sun dried tomatoes, about two ounces (two ounces is enough to use in a dish serving four people).

Baked goods

Bagels: You may have frozen bagels in the freezer. If not, buy some fresh or frozen bagels. (Freeze leftover bagels immediately.)

Bread: By now, you have a pattern of bread use, so buy what you will need

Brownies: make or purchase some brownies. Don't forget to purchase baking chocolate if starting from scratch.

Cookies: Buy or bake some, using one of the recipes in this book. Or buy fresh cookie dough, from the dairy section of the market.

Coffee cake: See frozen foods, above.

English muffins: Purchase some of these, if you are using a lot of baked goods.

Hamburger rolls or buns: buy enough for Saturday's dinner, if using barbecued hamburger menu.

Pie crust. One ready to bake pie crust from the baking supplies section. (Not needed if you purchase your pumpkin pie.)

Canned or bottled goods

Artichoke hearts: one 6.5 ounce jar of marinated artichoke hearts.

Asparagus: a one pound can of asparagus spears, if you are not going to use fresh asparagus.

Beverages: Check the supply of beverages you intend to serve, (hard liquor, beer, wine, soft drinks, juices, punch, bottled waters).

Chicken: 1 seven ounce can chicken, for the chicken salad recipe.

Chocolate sauce: Get one can of sauce, such as Hershey's.

Cranberry sauce: One can cranberry sauce, if not making it fresh.

Olives: One jar of green olives and one can of black olives (pitted).

Peanut butter: Check your supply and get more if needed.

Pickles: Check your larder to see if you have pickles, and catsup, mustard and relish as well.

Pumpkin pie filling. One 1 pound can of pumpkin pie filling. This is enough for one single crust pumpkin pie.

Tip Pumpkin pies and cream pies use a single crust beneath the filling. Fruit pies are often made with bottom top crusts.

Salsa: Get a jar of salsa for the big game; and some chips, too.

Salmon: One 16 ounce can of salmon for Thursday's lunch.

Soup: One can cream of asparagus soup.

Tomato sauce: 1 sixteen ounce can.

Tuna fish, 1 can.

Worcestershire sauce: If you don't already have this in your pantry, buy a small bottle.

Chapter Eleven

Menus and Recipes for Week Five

Monday

Breakfast: Melon and strawberries, cinnamon toast strips, tea or coffee.

Lunch: Ham and asparagus roll ups with Hollandaise sauce, Alice's potato salad, rolls and butter, cola drink, Larisa's strawberries with sour cream

Snack: Bread sticks with wedge of Swiss cheese, mineral water.

Dinner: Hamburger and rice stir-up, cauliflower and carrots, artichoke and tomato salad, bread and butter, beer or wine, coffee.

Tuesday

Breakfast: Red flannel eggs, juice, coffee or tea, fruit.

Lunch: Avocados stuffed with fruit salad, iced tea, rolls, butter, vanilla pudding with banana slices.

Snack: Tortilla chips and salsa, cola drink

Cocktail Party: At some point, you are going to be faced with having a cocktail party. This is how to do it, with minimum fuss.

Dinner: Chicken (or tuna or beef) pasta bake, green salad, bread or rolls with butter, coffee or tea, melon (or strawberries, blueberries, raspberries, or other fruit), with liqueur or milk.

Wednesday

Breakfast: Grapefruit half, bagel with cream cheese, coffee or tea.

Lunch: Hot pepper or Swiss cheese, tomato and lettuce sandwich on white toast

Snack: Plums, nectarine or other fresh fruit

Dinner: Vegetarian stuffed peppers with rice, Brussels sprouts or lima beans, bread and butter, pound cake with ice cream and chocolate sauce.

Thursday

Breakfast: Blueberry pancakes, sliced peaches or strawberries, coffee or tea

Lunch: Salmon patties with peas and white sauce, sliced potatoes

Snack: Peanut butter on crackers, apple

Dinner: Roast turkey with stuffing, baked potatoes, green beans, cranberry sauce, rolls and butter, white wine, sparkling water, pumpkin pie

Friday

Breakfast: Turkey hash with poached eggs, toast or English muffins, fruit or juice, coffee or tea

Lunch: Grilled tomato, corned beef (or use ham or sliced chicken) and mozzarella sandwiches, fruit cup, milk, pudding or gelatin dessert.

Snack: Orange or tangerine.

Dinner: Smothered veal chops with onions, sliced potatoes, spinach, bread and butter, fruit, coffee or tea.

Saturday

Breakfast: Baked peaches, or apples, cereal, toast, fruit or juice, coffee or tea.

Lunch: Sliced turkey with stuffing and gravy, broccoli, rice, bread and butter, coffee or tea

Snack: Apple sauce or whole apple

Dinner: Sole or whitefish, hash brown or baked potato, peas, celery, date and cheddar cheese salad.

Alternative menu: Barbecued hamburger on buns, French fries, lettuce and tomato, onion, beer, wine or soda, nectarines or apricots.

Sunday:

Breakfast: Scrambled eggs, fruit juice, toast or rolls, coffee or tea.

Lunch: Cream cheese and olive sandwiches or turkey salad sandwiches, iced tea or fruit punch, cookies or ice cream

Snack: Cheese spread with crackers

Hors d'ouevre: mini-salmon cakes

Dinner: The Big Game: buffet dinner for twelve people: baked ham; three pepper and mozzarella salad, potato salad, black bean, corn, and tomato salad, assorted breads, assorted relishes and condiments; beers, ales, and soft drinks, chips and dips, sheet cake, brownies, cookies, apples, coffee.

Monday. Week Five

Breakfast: Melon slices with fresh strawberries, Charlie's cinnamon toast strips, coffee or tea.

Melon slices with fresh strawberries

1 cantaloupe or honeydew melon, halved.
1 pint fresh strawberries that have been washed and hulled.
lemon juice (optional)

Remove seeds and pulp from melon. To serve four, cut each half in half again. Slice and peel if desired, or leave peel on and serve cut side up. Into the hollow left by the pulp, place some strawberries that have been washed and hulled. Sprinkle some fresh lemon juice onto the fruit, if desired.

Variation: substitute blueberries or raspberries for the strawberries.

Charlie's cinnamon toast strips

four slices toast, lightly buttered
small amount sugar
small amount cinnamon

If you're using regular bread, toast it and butter toast, then lightly sprinkle cinnamon and sugar on top of each slice. Cut each slice into strips. If you wish, brown it for about half a minute under the broiler, just enough to melt the butter and sugar together. If you're using cinnamon or cinnamon raisin bread, you may want to eliminate the additional cinnamon, and just use butter and sugar.

Variation: serve coffee cake instead of cinnamon toast strips.

Lunch

Ham and asparagus roll-ups with Hollandaise sauce, Alice's potato salad, bread and butter, iced tea.

Ham and asparagus roll ups with Hollandaise sauce

Asparagus is available fresh or canned.

16 spears fresh asparagus
8 slices cooked ham, sliced thin (from the deli department)
Hollandaise sauce, mock hollandaise sauce, white sauce or sauce made from condensed soup. (Sauce recipes follow.)
four slices of toast.

Preheat oven to 350° F. Wash asparagus and remove tough ends from bottom of each spear. Poach by placing asparagus in a skillet with water to cover and bringing to a boil, then reducing heat. Simmer for about five minutes, until tender. Remove from heat and drain. Cut ham slices in half lengthwise. Roll a half slice of ham around each asparagus spear. Heat in oven for five minutes, or until ham has been warmed through. Toast bread. Serve on toast, pouring hollandaise sauce over the ham and asparagus rolls. If using canned asparagus, skip the poaching step.

Hollandaise sauce

Hollandaise sauce is a mixture of egg yolks, melted butter and lemon juice. It is made in a double boiler (lower vessel holds water, upper vessel holds sauce) over a very low flame. If you do not have a double boiler, borrow one from a friend, or use one of the other sauces.

two egg yolks
1 stick butter, melted (makes 1/2 cup melted butter)
juice of 1/2 lemon

Separate the eggs, reserving the whites for another use. In the top of a double boiler, the bottom of which has water simmering over a low flame, place two uncooked egg yolks and begin whisking them. Very slowly add the melted butter, whisking continuously. The sauce will begin to thicken. Slowly add the lemon juice. Serve immediately.

Mock Hollandaise sauce

1 cup sour cream
1 stick butter, melted (makes 1/2 cup)
juice of 1/2 lemon

This sauce is easy. To 1 cup sour cream, add a little melted butter and some lemon juice.

White sauce (also known as Bechamel sauce)

For some reason, this sauce has fallen out of favor, but it is quite good and really easy to prepare. There are a number of ways to make white sauce. The from "scratch" way involves blending flour and melted butter over medium heat into a mixture called a "roux" and then adding milk or milk and stock. A much easier white-type sauce is made by blending a "cream of" some flavor condensed soup with about half of a soup can (5 to 6 ounces) of milk.

1/2 stick butter, melted (makes about 1/4 cup)
2 Tbs. flour
1/2 cup milk

Melt the butter in a small saucepan, and add 1 Tbs. of the flour, stirring constantly, until blended. Add the second Tbs. of the flour, and cook, gently, for about three minutes. Slowly add the milk, and heat, stirring constantly, until the sauce is thickened. Additional milk may be added for a thinner sauce.

Sauce made from cream of asparagus soup

This is by far the easiest white-type sauce to make.

1 10 and 1/2 ounce can cream of asparagus soup
1/2 of soup can milk
few drops lemon juice

Place contents of soup can in saucepan and slowly add a half soup can of milk, stirring constantly over low heat. When the sauce is done, stir a few drops of lemon juice into the sauce.

Alice's potato salad

1 pound redskin potatoes
1 red onion, cut up
3 or 4 TBS nonfat mayonnaise (optional: regular mayonnaise)
Salt and pepper

Alice says the simpler, the better. Wash potatoes but do not peel, and boil until tender. Cut into bite sized pieces. Toss with red onion pieces, mayonnaise and salt and pepper. Chill and serve.

Snack

Tortilla chips and salsa, and cold drink.

Dinner

Hamburger and rice stir-up, cauliflower and carrots, artichoke and tomato salad, bread and butter, beer or wine, coffee.

Cauliflower and carrots

1 head cauliflower or 1 box frozen cauliflower
1 half pound carrots, or 1 box frozen carrots

If using fresh vegetables, clean and cut them. Place in saucepan with small amount of water. Heat to boiling, then simmer five minutes. Can also be cooked in microwave. Serves four.

Hamburger and rice stir-up

1 medium onion, chopped
1 tsp. fennel seed, or 1 tsp rosemary, crushed
1 pound hamburger
2 cups cooked rice

Heat onion and fennel seed or rosemary over medium heat in skillet; when onions are translucent, add ground beef. Stir to break the meat into small pieces. Brown thoroughly. Add the cooked rice, and continue cooking until all ingredients are hot.

Tuesday, Week Five

Breakfast

Red flannel eggs, juice, coffee or tea, fruit.

Red flannel eggs

4 English muffin halves (use 2 English muffins)
4 slices cooked corned beef, turkey, or ham (from deli counter if you do not have leftovers available)
1/4 cup chopped onions
1 large baking potato, sliced and sauteed, *or* one 15 oz. can sliced potatoes, drained and rinsed.
4 eggs, uncooked
1 eight ounce can tomato sauce
hot pepper sauce, such as Tabasco

Preheat oven to 375° F. Saute onion and potato slices on medium heat until onions are translucent and potatoes are tender. Toast and lightly butter each English muffin half. In each of four small baking dishes. place an English muffin half topped with one slice meat, followed by some potato and onion mixture, a dash of hot pepper sauce, and some tomato sauce, reserving about four tsps. Break one egg into each dish.Top with 1 tsp. of the tomato sauce. Bake for twenty minutes, or until eggs are done. Serves four.

Lunch

Avocado halves stuffed with fruit salad, iced tea, rolls butter, vanilla pudding with banana slices.

Avocado halves with fruit salad

2 avocados, halved.
2 Tbs. lemon juice mixed into water

Halve avocados and remove pits. Immerse into lemon juice and water mixture to keep from blackening. Stuff with fruit salad (recipe follows). Serves four.

Fruit salad

This is a very flexible salad. Use your imagination to combine interesting and tasty fruits. You want to wind up with about two cups of fruit salad. Use fruit that is pretty, and that provides good textural and color contrasts. For example, you might use:

1 apple, washed, cored, and cut up
1 plum, washed, pitted and cut up
1 orange, peeled, pitted and cut into sections
1/2 cup white grapes
2 Tbs. mayonnaise
2 Tbs. sour cream

Toss first four ingredients together. Mix mayonnaise and sour cream well, and toss with fruit. Stuff avocados with salad until the salad overflows the avocados, to create an abundant appearance. Garnish with parsley. Serve on lettuce leaves. Serves four.

Variation: no time? Use canned fruit cocktail instead of fruit salad. or buy fruit salad from the deli department .

Snack

Tortilla chips with salsa. Cold drink.

Cocktail Party

By now, you have the experience to throw a cocktail party for twelve to eighteen people. First, estimate the number of guests and figure on three to four drinks per person, and six to eight appetizers or *hors d'ouevres* per individual. Have at least twice as many glasses on hand as guests. You can rent glasses and plates from rental companies, if you do not own a sufficient number. Or buy plastic or paper items.

Beverages

What beverages do you plan to serve? If it is a party where you intend to offer hard liquor, wine and beer, have on hand three to four bottles each of red and white wine, two or three six packs of beer, and a 750 ml bottle of each of vodka, gin, Scotch, Bourbon, and rum. Buy 1 liter of mixers for each three people you expect, and include ginger ale, tonic water, club soda, and regular sparkling water (seltzer) in the array. Conservatively, this will provide 172 servings. Some of this will be left over. But you will be regarded as a generous and thoughtful host.

Before your party, starting now, look about you. At parties you attend, what are people drinking? If certain beverages are more popular among your friends or in the region that you are living, adjust your stock of beverages accordingly. Generally, gin and rum are the two liquors that are ordered least. You may live in an area where blended,Rye or Canadian whiskey are popular, and if so, get a bottle of that. They are technically not the same, but generally people who ask for blended or Rye whiskeys, will drink Canadian.

Non-alcoholic drinks

Be sure to have an assortment of non-alcoholic beverages, since more people are drinking in moderation or not at all. Various waters such as Perrier or Pellegrino are popular, as are juices, punches, diet beverages, and soft drinks.

Accompaniments

If you are planning on a full bar, have some cocktail cherries, fresh lemon slices, lime slices, and cocktail onions and green stuffed olives available. If your crowd likes Martinis and Manhattans, you will also need small bottles of dry and sweet vermouth. These drinks are usually mixed at a ratio of three liquor (gin or vodka for Martinis, made with dry vermouth, and bourbon or blended whiskey for Manhattans, made with sweet vermouth) to one vermouth, but many folks will ask for them dryer (less vermouth).

Food

Always offer food at cocktail parties. People really appreciate appetizers or *hors d'ouevres* at cocktail parties, even if they don't tell you so. Foods you do not need to prepare include mixed nuts, peanuts, potato and other chips, dips, and pretzels. You can purchase some frozen appetizers, and heat them up; prepare some of the appetizer recipes from this book, or have a caterer come in (this last option can be expensive).

Bartending, supplies, and ice

If you are having more than twelve people, ask a friend to help with the drinks, or make the bar self-service; or hire a bartender (again, this can get costly, but really makes life convenient). Have plenty of napkins, drink stirrers, paper or plastic plates, ash trays, and some paper towels on hand. The same friend (or you yourself) should make a couple of "sweeps" of the room during the party to pick up used glasses, plates, and anything else that has been discarded by the guests. One final note: have enough ice. Buy some in advance or make some. You will need one ice cube tray (about one pound) of ice per person, more in hot weather. Clear space in your freezer to store the ice. Have a great party!

Dinner

Chicken pasta bake, tossed green salad, bread or rolls and butter, coffee or tea, strawberries with brown sugar and sour cream.

Chicken pasta bake

1 large chicken breast, unsplit (or two cups cooked chicken, diced)
1/2 pound shell or elbow macaroni
1 10 and 1/2 ounce can condensed cream of chicken soup
1/2 soup can water, milk, broth, or white wine
1 rib celery, diced
1 Tbs. lemon juice
1 medium onion, chopped
1/2 stick butter
1/8 cup chopped fresh parsley or 2 Tbs. parsley flakes, divided

Preheat oven to 375° F. Brown chicken breasts in skillet (no need to brown cooked chicken). Cut into bite sized pieces. Cook and drain pasta following package directions. Mix soup, water, chicken, pasta, soup, celery, half the parsley, and lemon juice. Bake in greased 9 x 13 inch casserole for 1 hour or until bubbling. Sprinkle remaining parsley on finished dish and serve. Serves six.

Green salad with orange juice dressing

6 spinach leaves, washed and torn up
6 Romaine or bibb lettuce leaves, or mixture, washed and torn up

Mix greens, and toss with orange juice dressing (recipe below).

Orange juice dressing

3 Tbs. olive oil
1 Tbs. white vinegar or 1 Tbs. lemon juice
1 Tbs. orange juice.

Mix well and toss with salad.

Larisa's strawberries with brown sugar and sour cream

32 strawberries, washed but not hulled
1/2 cup sour cream
4 Tbs. brown sugar, crumbled

Use four plates. Place sour cream in the center, surrounded by brown sugar. Place strawberries around edges of each plate. Dip each strawberry in the sour cream, then the sugar. Serves four.

Wednesday, Week Five

Breakfast

Grapefruit half, bagel with cream cheese, coffee or tea.

Lunch

Hot pepper cheese, tomato and lettuce sandwiches on toast

two slices white toast
two slices hot pepper cheese
tomato and lettuce slices
mayonnaise

Spread mayonnaise on toast, layer lettuce, cheese, and tomato. Cover with second slice of toast. Place on luncheon plate; garnish with olives and pickles, and serve.

Snack

Plums, nectarine or other fresh fruit

Dinner

Vegetarian stuffed peppers with rice, Brussels sprouts, rolls and butter, coffee or tea, pound cake with chocolate sauce, ice cream.

Vegetarian stuffed peppers with rice

four green bell peppers, washed, cored, and seeded, with tops removed (other colors may be substituted)
two cups cooked rice
one 4 ounce can mushrooms or eight ounces fresh mushrooms
one 8 ounce package shredded cheddar or mozzarella cheese
one 4 ounce jar chopped pimentos
one egg, lightly beaten

Preheat oven to 350°F. Mix first five ingredients together, then mix in beaten egg. Stuff peppers and place upright in baking dish. Bake for one hour or until top of stuffing is browned. Serves four.

Brussels sprouts

1 box frozen Brussels sprouts

Microwave them or heat in a saucepan, with small amount water.

Pound cake with chocolate sauce and ice cream

one 1 lb. pound cake, frozen or from bakery
chocolate sauce (recommended: Hershey's)
ice cream.

Drizzle chocolate sauce on pound cake slices, top with ice cream.

Thursday, Week Five

Breakfast

Blueberry pancakes, sliced peaches or strawberries, coffee or tea.

Blueberry pancakes

Make pancakes from pancake or baking mix. When batter has been mixed, add 3/4 cup blueberries and prepare as usual.

Sliced peaches

1 peach per person.

Slice peaches, and serve with a little milk, or some liqueur.

Note: Fresh peaches are available only during a relatively short period of the summer. When they are not available, use frozen or canned peaches..

Lunch

Salmon patties with peas and white sauce, rosemary potatoes. Bread and butter, coffee, or tea, fruit or ice cream.

Salmon patties with peas, white sauce and sliced potatoes

This is an old recipe, dating back to when most of the households in America cooked extensively with canned foods. The canned peas have been replaced with frozen, which generally taste better.

one 16 ounce can salmon, or 2 cups cooked salmon, deboned and flaked
1 rib celery, minced finely
1 medium onion, minced finely
1 cup bread crumbs.
1 egg, lightly beaten
chopped parsley, to taste
1 box frozen peas.
2 hard cooked eggs, peeled and sliced (optional)

Mix salmon, celery, onion, and bread crumbs together. Add the beaten egg. Lightly fry the patties to brown them. Place in a baking dish and bake fifteen to twenty minutes, or until done. Meanwhile, prepare the white sauce and mix with the peas. Heat until warm. If using the hard cooked eggs, slice and add them to the white sauce. Serve white sauce over the salmon patties. Serves four.

Rosemary Potatoes

Four medium potatoes, or one can sliced potatoes,
Rosemary
Olive oil or other oil, for sauteing

Wash and slice potatoes. Heat 2 Tbs. of oil in a skillet, on medium heat. When oil is hot, add potatoes, sprinkling generously with rosemary. Cook until brown and crispy.

Snack

Peanut butter on crackers, apple

Dinner

Roast turkey with stuffing, baked potatoes, green beans, cranberry sauce, rolls and butter, white wine, sparkling water, pumpkin pie

Note: This dinner usually means more guests and a bit more work than usual. Manage the work by doing some advance planning. For example, set the table the night before. Bake the pie the day before or use a frozen pumpkin pie, which can warm up in the oven while everyone eats dinner. Cranberry sauce is easy to prepare, and can be done days before. Use brown and serve rolls. The ingredients for the stuffing can be washed and chopped the day before, and mixed on the day the turkey is stuffed and baked.

Green beans

Use green beans recipe from Monday, Week One (p. 65).

Heads up for Roast turkey:

1. If serving a whole turkey, buy it several days before roasting and thaw it in the refrigerator, in a large basin or dishpan;

2. Be sure to read the directions on the turkey wrapper and follow them carefully;

3. Usually, the gizzards (heart, liver, etc.) are inside the turkey in a small paper bag and need to be removed;

4. Often, the legs are fixed together with a plastic or metal holder that needs to be removed;

5. Most turkeys come with the neck severed and placed inside the body cavity; be sure to remove it.

6. Rinse the turkey well under cold running water and dry it with paper towels;

7. Don't stuff the turkey until ready to put it into the oven.

Roast turkey

1 frozen turkey

Preheat oven to 375°F. Be certain to follow directions on the wrapper the turkey cam in and to observe the **Heads up** that precedes this recipe (p. 223). Rub the turkey all over with melted butter or margarine or salad oil; stuff the turkey (dressing recipe follows) Place turkey in a large roasting pan and put into the oven. Bake for 20 minutes per pound. If top of turkey gets too brown, place aluminum foil over the top of the turkey to stop browning. After removing the turkey from the oven, let it "rest" for about ten minutes before carving.

Stuffing (also known as dressing)

1 bag bread stuffing mix (should say enough for a 14 pound turkey)
1 medium onion, chopped
2 ribs celery, chopped
1/4 cup chopped fresh parsley
1 stick butter or margarine, melted
2 cans low sodium or regular chicken broth

Place dry ingredients in bowl, and add liquid ingredients. Mix well. Add a little water or white wine if too dry. Stuff the large cavity of the bird; if there is stuffing remaining, stuff the neck cavity. If there is still stuffing left over, bake it in a glass or metal baking dish when you bake the turkey, but remove it after about one hour, or when the top of the stuffing has browned.

Variations: There are many variations on turkey stuffings. Some old recipes call for oysters and chestnuts (shell the oysters and roast and peel the chestnuts first!), while others are based on corn bread, and have sage, sausage and hot pepper added. Apples and raisins are other ingredients that frequently turn up in bread stuffing. If you ask around, you will discover that no two people make stuffing quite the same way. Many recipes call for more butter and less broth than the recipe used here.

Baked potatoes

one russet (Idaho) potato per person, washed but not peeled

Place potatoes in the oven. Bake about 1-1/2 hours, or until done.

Cranberry sauce

one pound cranberries (sold fresh or frozen)
3/4 to 1 cup sugar
2 cups water.

Rinse cranberries, place in saucepan with water and sugar over medium heat, and boil until cranberries burst. Place in serving dish and cool. If making ahead, refrigerate until using.

Time-saver: Use canned cranberry sauce instead.

Pumpkin pie

one 9-inch, refrigerated unbaked pie crust
one 15 ounce can pumpkin pie filling (enough for 1 pie)
one 15 ounce can sweetened condensed milk
2 eggs, lightly beaten
1 teaspoon ground cinnamon
1/2 teaspoon ground ginger
1/2 teaspoon ground nutmeg
1/2 teaspoon salt (optional)

Preheat oven to 425°F. Mix all ingredients in a large bowl, and pour into pie crust. Bake 15 minutes at 425°, then reduce oven temperature to 350°. Bake another 35 to 40 minutes, or until knife inserted in center of pie comes out clean.

Serving suggestion: serve with whipped cream or ice cream.

Friday, Week Five

Breakfast

Turkey hash with poached eggs, toast or English muffins, fruit or juice, coffee or tea

Turkey hash with poached eggs

1/2 medium onion, chopped
1 cup leftover turkey, cubed
1 cup leftover potatoes, diced
chopped parsley, if desired

Heat some shortening or oil in a frying pan and cook the onion until soft. Mix remaining ingredients together and fry, until onion is cooked and mixture is crisp. Serve with poached eggs.

Poached eggs

Use poached eggs recipe from Wednesday, Week Two (page 116).

Lunch

Grilled tomato and mozzarella sandwiches, fruit cup, milk, pudding or gelatin dessert

Snack

Orange or tangerine

Dinner

Veal chops smothered in onions, sliced potatoes, spinach, rolls and butter, coffee and tea, fruit.

Veal chops "smothered" in onions

2 onions, chopped
four veal chops
sliced potatoes
sage or rosemary, to taste

Heat oil in frying pan and cook onions until translucent. Add veal chops and brown on one side, then reduce heat. Turn and cook until veal is well done. Pile onions on top of veal chops, and serve.

Sliced potatoes

1 can sliced potatoes

Rinse and drain potatoes in colander. Place single layer of potatoes in skillet used for the veal and heat, turning each slice once. Repeat until all potatoes cook. Serve with veal and onions.

Spinach

1 box frozen spinach or 1 package fresh spinach

Heat frozen spinach in saucepan or microwave until hot. If using fresh spinach, wash first. Drain, then cook until tender.

Variation: Garnish with chopped hard boiled egg.

Saturday, Week Five

Breakfast

Hot cereal, fruit or juice, toast and butter, coffee or tea

Baked pears or peaches

eight pear or peach halves, canned or fresh
brown sugar or maple syrup, to taste
water

Preheat oven to 350°F. Place fresh peaches, skin side down in a baking dish in about 1 inch of water, add brown sugar. Bake one hour. For canned peaches, bake 1/2 hour.

Lunch

Leftover turkey: sliced turkey with stuffing and gravy, broccoli, rice, bread and butter, coffee or tea

Leftover turkey

Heat the leftover turkey and stuffing, and the gravy. Use one of the broccoli recipes from Friday, Week One (pp. 89-90).

Snack

Apple sauce or whole apple

Dinner

Sole or whitefish, hash brown or baked potatoes, peas, celery, date and cheddar cheese salad.

Alternative menu: Barbecued hamburger on buns, French fries, lettuce and tomato, onion, beer, wine or soda, nectarines or apricots

Sole or whitefish

1 pound sole, flounder, or other boneless white fish filets
poaching liquid made of 1/3 water, 1/3 stock, 1/3 white wine, in sufficient quantity to cover fish (start with about 2 cups)

Preheat oven to 350° F. Rinse fish, pat dry with paper towels and place in glass or metal baking dish. Cover with poaching liquid. Poach 1/2 hour, or until opaque and fork tender. Serves four.

Barbecued hamburger

one pound ground beef
1/2 onion, chopped
1/4 tsp. garlic powder or 1 clove finely chopped garlic
1/2 tsp. ground hot pepper
1 cup commercial barbecue sauce

Mix ingredients together and pan fry or grill. Cover with barbecue sauce. Serve with French fries.

Baked or hash brown potatoes

For baked, use potato recipe from Monday, Week One (p. 64). **For hash browns, use** 1 package frozen hash brown potatoes. Prepare potatoes according to directions on package. The potatoes will require more cooking time than the fish.

Date, celery, and cheddar cheese salad

2 ribs celery
12 dates, pitted and split
four slices cheddar cheese or other sharp cheese
balsalmic vinegar
olive oil
salt and pepper

Slowly saute celery in frying pan until tender (this takes about 20 minutes). Cut into sticks, and arrange on salad plates with dates. Drizzle vinegar and oil over celery and dates. Season to taste. Top with sharp cheddar cheese. Serves four.

Sunday, Week Five

Breakfast

Scrambled eggs, fruit juice, toast or rolls, coffee or tea.

Lunch

Cream cheese and olive sandwiches or turkey salad sandwiches, iced tea or fruit punch, cookies or ice cream

For turkey salad sandwiches, follow the recipe for tuna salad sandwiches from Tuesday, Week One (p. 68).

Cream cheese and olive sandwiches

For each sandwich, you will need

2 slices bread
softened cream cheese
eight green or black olives, pitted
small amount chopped celery

Mix cream cheese, olives, and celery together. Spread on one slice bread, top with second slice, cut diagonally in half, and serve.

Fruit punch

Buy fruit punch, such as Hawaiian Punch, or mix 1 pint iced tea, 1 pint orange juice, and 1/2 cup crushed strawberries. Serves four.

Snack

Cheese spread with crackers

Use commercial cheese spread or mix softened cream cheese with finely chopped onion and parsley, and a dash garlic powder.

Hors d'ouevres or appetizer

Mini-salmon cakes. (Since dinner is The Big Game, this appetizer can be served with the dinner)

Mini-salmon cakes

The difference between salmon patties, (Thursday, Week Five, p. 222) and these mini-salmon cakes is slight. The mini-salmon cakes are smaller in size, and somewhat spicier; the amount of bread crumbs is reduced; and the peas and white sauce are not used. Since the mini-salmon cake recipe is for appetizer portions, this recipe serves eight rather than four.

one 16 ounce can salmon, or 2 cups cooked salmon, deboned and flaked
1 rib celery, minced finely
1 medium onion, minced finely
1/2 cup bread crumbs.
1 egg, lightly beaten
chopped parsley, to taste
1/4 tsp. ground red pepper, or to taste
1/4 tsp. garlic powder, or to taste

Preheat oven to 350° F. Mix salmon, celery, onion, and bread crumbs together, adding beaten egg and seasonings. Shape into small cakes and fry the cakes to brown them, then place in baking dish and bake 15 minutes or until done. Serves eight as appetizer.

Dinner

The Big Game: buffet dinner for 12 people: baked ham; three pepper and mozzarella salad, potato salad, black bean, corn, and tomato salad, assorted breads, assorted relishes and condiments; beers, ales, and soft drinks, chips and dips, sheet cake, brownies, cookies, apples, coffee. Since you want to have fun with your guests, the secret to this dinner is to make it easy on yourself. Casual is the word, and today is the day for paper or plastic plates, plastic drinking cups or glasses, and plastic flatware. Depending on how informal the event is going to be, you might even want to invest in a throwaway paper or plastic tablecloth and paper napkins and accessories.

Tip: Make a list of non-food items you will be using and pick them up well in advance of the party.

Tip: Figure one tray of ice cubes per person, or about 12 pounds of ice for 12 people. Use more ice if the weather is hot, or if you are serving canned and bottled drinks in a tub of ice.

About ham

You've got a lot of options. Talk to your butcher and also to your friends who've prepared hams. Hams are available cooked and uncooked, sliced and unsliced, smoked, or not smoked, and in various sizes. Many cities have stores that sell cooked, "spiral sliced" hams. These are expensive, but very convenient and tasty. Ham on the bone is somewhat more atmospheric, if a bit more difficult to serve. You'll probably want to heat or bake it, to serve warm or at room temperature, unless the game you're watching is being televised in midsummer. Some popular ham options:

Uncooked fresh ham. Figure on one half-pound per person, plus a pound or so of bone, if you purchase a ham with bone-in. An eight pound ham should do it for twelve people. Fresh hams are unsmoked and need to be baked thoroughly.

Country ham. These are hams cured in smokehouses and that are usually highly salted. Follow package directions; often these directions call for soaking the ham in water for 24 hours or overnight. These hams are highly regarded for their strong flavor. They don't require cooking but often are served heated.

Hickory smoked ham. This sort of ham, also cured in smokehouses, is prepared in many regions and is often sold ready to eat. They usually are less salty than country hams. The hams will generally have a hickory (or other hardwood, such as maple) flavor.

Baked canned unsmoked hams. These hams are sold in markets. The canned hams have been cooked in the can at high temperatures. Usually these hams are boneless. They are easy to slice and ready to serve right out of the can, but do not have as good a texture as hams that have not been canned.

Baked hams, uncanned. Many stores and butcher shops sell these hams. They are precooked and frequently pre-sliced.

Tip: Bake uncooked hams for 20 minutes per pound at 350° F. Precooked hams will require less cooking time.

Baked beans

Use the baked beans recipe from Sunday, Week Three (p. 158), tripled. Makes 12 servings. Or, serve hearty baked beans:

Hearty baked beans

three 15 ounce cans of baked beans (with pork, or vegetarian)
3 Tbs. catsup
3 Tbs. molasses or 3 Tbs. brown sugar
four to eight slices cooked bacon, crumbled
1/4 cup finely chopped onion.

Preheat oven to 350° F. Mix all ingredients. Bake 30 minutes. Serves 12.

Three pepper and mozzarella salad

two red bell peppers, washed cored, and sliced into thin strips
two green bell peppers, washed, cored, and sliced into thin strips
two yellow bell peppers, washed, cored and sliced into thin strips
1/2 pound mozzarella cheese, sliced and cut into thin strips
1/4 cup olive oil
1/4 cup chopped fresh basil, or 1 Tbs. dried basil

Mix ingredients together, tossing well. Serve at room temperature. May be made several hours prior to serving and refrigerated.

Potato salad

Use the recipe for Alice's potato salad from Monday, Week Five (p. 215), or the recipe for hot potato salad from Sunday, Week Three (p. 159). Or buy some potato salad from the deli. Figure about 1/4 pound of potato salad per person.

Black bean, corn, and tomato salad

This salad uses black beans and corn, tomatoes, and green onions for yellow, red, and green accents. Serve at room temperature.

three 15 ounce cans black beans, drained and rinsed
two medium tomatoes, pulp and seeds removed, diced
one 16 ounce can corn, drained
one bunch green onions (scallions) washed, and chopped
1/4 cup olive oil or salad oil
1 Tbs. vinegar or lemon juice (optional)
1/4 tsp cayenne pepper or ground red pepper (optional)
Mix first four ingredients together, tossing gently with olive oil. Add vinegar or lemon juice and hot pepper, if desired. Toss again. Place in serving dish. Serve at room temperature. Serves twelve.

Pickles, olives, condiments

Bring out some pickles, pitted black olives, green olives, mustard and catsup, salt and pepper and place on the buffet table.

Sheet cake

Buy a sheet cake at the supermarket, or bake a mix cake, in a 9 x 13 inch baking dish. Check the cake mix boxes carefully, as you may need two boxes of cake mix. Generally, a cake mix for a two layer cake will do well in a 9 x 13 inch baking dish, and will make one layer. Cool, and frost. Use a can of prepared frosting.

Brownies

Buy some, or use a mix, or Tuesday, Week One recipe (p. 69).

Fruit punch

If you are planning to serve fruit punch, triple the Fruit punch recipe on p. 227.

Tip: Don't forget coffee, tea, cream, sugar, and other items you'll need at the end of the party.

Chapter 12

Additional Recipes and Cleaning Up

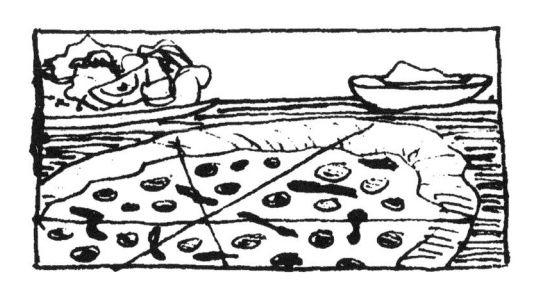

THE MEAL is over and now there is a pile of dirty dishes, pots, and pans in the sink. Or perhaps there already was a pile of dirty dishes, pots, and pans in the sink and now that pile is bigger. What to do? Easy: clean 'em up. Think in terms of overall strategies; big jobs; and everyday items.

Reading about cleanup can seem overwhelming. In practice, we're talking about 15 minutes to a half-hour per night, once you have a system in place that you like. If there are more than one of you, why not work out a system where the cleanup is shared?

The necessity of keeping your kitchen clean is not a new problem. A famous comedienne used to describe her culinary life by discussing the time she had a grease fire--in her sink. There are a number of basic strategies for approaching this problem, some more sensible than others, and numerous good methods and techniques for actually dealing with it.

Overall strategies

Strategy 1:

This strategy avoids the question entirely. You simply use disposable cookware, such as single use muffin tins and roasting pans; disposable dishes and cups; and disposable flatware. This strategy has its advantages at large parties and picnics, for example. It also comes in handy when cleanup facilities are limited, such as in offices. On a day-to-day basis in your home, it tends to get expensive. Also, constant use of disposables tends to become somewhat esthetically limiting. Even truck stops use real dishes.

Strategy 2:

A second (and perhaps more common) strategy is to leave all objects that need washing in the sink, or just around, until there are no clean kitchen objects left in one's home. At that point, strategy 2's very real disadvantages become painfully obvious, and any previous advantage of strategy 2 (the sublime convenience of procrastination) is long forgotten. While some folks follow this strategy, we do not recommend it.

Strategy 3:

This is the polar opposite of Strategy 2. Clean like mad. Make cleaning your kitchen your new mission in life. Each Saturday morning, scour every metal object in your kitchen. Wash down the kitchen walls each night, and stop several times during the food preparation process to thoroughly clean everything in sight.

Whisk dishes and flatware away from diners as soon as they have finished eating, or even before they have finished, and loudly rinse and stack them so everyone will know how efficient and clean you are. If you have an automatic dishwasher, start running it right during the meal. Put it on the loudest cycle, to telegraph your thoroughness. Unless you are a hermit, you will discover that this strategy is not likely to increase your popularity. Although Strategy 3 is preferable to Strategy 2, it isn't one that many people adopt.

Strategy 4:

Move out of your apartment and start over. This is known as the geographical solution. Or, to expend even less effort, you might consider becoming a possum. The relocation approach has been used in some extreme situations, but even if this step is something you are contemplating, you might as well read this chapter anyway, since it will prevent the problem from recurring in your next apartment.

While all of the foregoing have some advantages, they also have major disadvantages. We recommend:

Strategy 5:

In Strategy 5, there are many advantages and very few disadvantages. Clean *smarter* rather than *harder*. Choose methods and practices that maximize mealtime enjoyment and minimize long, boring cleanups. Some of them include: cleaning up on an as-you-go basis where it makes sense; focused reuse of certain preparation items; soaking the tough clean-up items to make them easier to clean; and use of good tools and supplies. This kind of planning and focus makes cleanup as rapid and effective as possible. After a time, it becomes automatic. It is this strategy that the author recommends, but you, gentle reader, probably already knew that.

Organized is better

All right, let's say we're going with Strategy 5 as the main strategy, with occasional forays into strategy 1. Look around the kitchen. Some things are already apparent to you, or you wouldn't be reading this book. Organized is better than disorganized; presentable is better than revolting; clean is better than dirty. Now: how to make it happen.

Begin with the refrigerator

Once every week, go through the refrigerator and toss out those things that are beyond their freshness date, clean up any spills, and generally, spruce the refrigerator interior up a bit, with a damp paper towel.

Floor care

Once every week, do the following: 1. mop the kitchen floor. Use one of those sponge mops and a bucket and a basic cleaner, such as Formula 479. After you mop the floor, go over it with a wrung out mop to get rid of excess water. Let the floor air dry.

Once a day, sweep the floor. Use a broom and dustpan, sweep up the crumbs and anything else that has fallen to the floor, and put the refuse in the trash. Most municipalities now require trash to be placed in plastic trash bags. Even if yours doesn't specifically require this, it is a good practice.

Trash and garbage

Some municipalities prohibit the disposal of garbage and require in-sink disposers. If you have an in-sink garbage disposer, by all means, use it. Wet garbage, such as coffee grounds, eggshells, and old cabbage, can be put through this appliance, which grinds up wet garbage and disposes of it into the sewage or septic system. If you do not have one, you might consider getting one; meanwhile the garbage portion of your refuse should be placed in plastic bags. Check with your municipality to determine what ordinances apply where you live.

Trash and garbage should be emptied every couple of days at a minimum. If it is to be held longer than that, it should be bagged in plastic bags and tightly sealed.

Putting food away minimizes pests

Don't leave food around. Put unused food back in its box, container, canister, or leftover dish. After you are through using a particular item, such as flour, close the cover on the canister and put the flour back where it belongs. Do this with all of the food you use, and particularly with items requiring refrigeration, such as dairy products.

Heads up: never leave food out overnight; it is a sure way to attract bugs and develop harmful bacteria.

It is always a good idea to clear plates and wash the dishes after each meal. If this is not possible, at least scrape and rinse the dishes, and stack them. This makes the ultimate cleanup a lot easier.

Clean as you go

One woman back in college had been in a 4-H club and had been taught to clean up as she went along in food preparations. She did this fairly automatically, and her kitchen always seemed pretty neat. After dinner, there wasn't as much work to do--a pretty good benefit.

Benefits of a good soak

If you don't have an automatic dishwasher, you will find that soaking items with crusts on them, such as a frying pan or roasting pan will make those items easier to clean. Lay in a supply of plastic scouring pads (these do not scratch); sponges; liquid dish detergent for small jobs; a detergent for automatic dishwashers if you have one; and some dish cloths to make your work easier.

Soaps and detergents

Keep liquid dish detergent, hand soap, and powdered dishwasher detergent (if you have an automatic dishwasher) on hand. Pick up a couple of plastic scouring pads, one or two sponges, a couple of dish cloths, and some dish towels. These should see you through virtually all dish, china, and pots and pans cleaning.

Prioritize the dirty dishes

For those who are going to be doing dishes by hand, using a basin of soapy water, try this method: do the cleanest items first, like water glasses, then work to the plates, the flatware, the pots and pans last. Change the dishwater if it gets too greasy.

Drainboards and dish racks help dishes dry

A dish draining rack and drainboard are good items to have if you are washing dishes manually. Returning the glasses, flatware, dishes, cups, saucers, and pots and pans to their shelves and cupboards is a good practice. Everything is then where you need it when you need it.

Here are some additional tips:

Tip: Stay in the kitchen while you are working. Many cooking fires are caused by unattended cooking.

Tip: Turn handles on pans and pots so that they do not stick out over the stove. When the handles on pots and pans are turned inward, you minimize the chance of spills and accidents.

Tip: Put things away as you finish using them. If the first stage of a recipe calls for milk, for example, measure out the quantity you need and return the milk container to the refrigerator. This gives you more work room, keeps the milk cold and fresh, and minimizes the risk of spills.

Additional recipes

Here are some additional recipes, in no particular order. They are terrific recipes, but did not fit into the five week menu plan.

Euro- breakfast

French or Italian bread, sliced
Asiago, provolone, or blue cheese, about four ounces
orange slices from two oranges
seedless red grapes

Slice the bread and cover with towel until ready to serve. Peel and slice the oranges, placing them in a dish. Place the cheese on a dish with a cheese knife. Wash the grapes and place on a dish. Let each person serve themselves from the serving dishes. Serve with espresso, coffee, or tea.

Chicken cacciatore (Chicken hunter style)

This recipe can be prepared partially on the stove top and partially in the oven. If using boneless chicken, use 1 and 1/2 pounds of boneless chicken thighs or breasts.

1 chicken, about 2 and 1/2 pounds, cut up into eight pieces
two medium green bell peppers
two medium onions
1/2 pound mushrooms
1 28 ounce can chopped or crushed tomatoes
1 bay leaf
parsley, oregano and/or basil, to taste
1/4 cup olive oil, for sauteing onions, peppers, and browning chicken
salt and pepper to taste

Preheat oven to 375° F. Saute onions, then peppers, followed by chicken, in cast iron frying pan. When chicken is brown, add mushrooms, tomatoes, and spices. Bake in frying pan for 90 minutes.

Broccoli and apple salad

This is a very refreshing salad that contains no added salt.

1 10 ounce frozen broccoli, cooked; or 1 cup cooked fresh broccoli, chopped
1/2 medium red onion, chopped
2 small apples, such as Jonathan or Winesap, or 1 large apple, such as Granny Smith, unpeeled but washed, cored and cut up
4 or 5 medium to large strawberries, washed, cored and cut up into slices
2 Tbs. flavored vinegar, such as malt, raspberry or cider vinegar
2 Tbs. olive oil
black pepper

Chop the broccoli, onion, apples, and strawberries and mix together in a large bowl. Toss with the vinegar, then add the oil and toss again. Sprinkle to taste with black pepper. Serves four.

Mashed potatoes and carrots

2 carrots, washed, with tops removed (peeling is optional) and cut up
2 large baking potatoes, washed and cut up (peeling optional)
1/4 cup milk, or more, if desired
butter, to taste
salt, to taste
pepper, to taste

Place carrots and potatoes together in a large pot with water about one inch over the tops of the vegetables. Boil the carrots and potatoes until they are cooked (fork will easily pierce them). Drain and add milk, and butter if desired. Mash together. Season to taste. Serves four.

Low fat and low salt alternative: use skim milk; delete the butter and salt. Add one or two Tbs. of the cooking liquid to the vegetables. The starch in the cooking liquid will make the vegetables creamier.

Variation: add chopped fresh parsley to the potatoes and carrots.

Variation: turnips can be substituted for the potatoes. Turnips can be found in supermarket produce department; unlike many vegetables, turnips do need to be peeled ; after peeling, they can be boiled in the same manner as potatoes.

Recipe Index

A

Alice's potato salad, 211
"Always There's"™ pasta with red sauce #2, 142
American spaghetti, 77
Apple sauce, 147
Artichoke dressing, 92
Asparagus spears, 146
Au gratin potatoes, 68
Avocado halves with fruit salad, 212

B

Bacon, 71
Bacon, lettuce and tomato sandwich, 148
Bacon burgers, 157
Bagels, 175
Baked apples, 65
Baked beans, 156
Baked peaches, 223
Baked pears, 167
Baked potatoes, 62
Barbecued hamburgers, 224
Bechamel sauce, 210
Beef stew (from scratch), 185
Beer coffee cake, 112
Beth's dressing, 125
Blue cheese stuffing, 159
Boiled rice, 93
Bologna, cheddar and tomato sandwich on hard roll, 154
Bow tie pasta with scallions, salmon and tomato, 1160
Brad's beer bread, 69
Bread and butter, 64
Breakfast bake, 148
Breakfast potatoes, 72
Broccoli, 87
Broccoli and apple salad, 237
Broiled tomatoes, 190
Brown gravy, 179
Brussels sprouts, 155

C

Carrot cake, 129
Carrot sticks, 61, 151
Carrots Csilla, 128
Cauliflower with carrots, 211
Ceil's Passover cookies, 177
Celery sticks and bell pepper rings, 121
Charlie's cinnamon toast strips, 175
Cheesecake, 112
Chicken artichoke bake, 94
Chicken bullion, 89
Chicken cacciatore, 237
Chicken livers, 183
Chicken pasta bake, 215
Chocolate pudding, 96
Coffee cookies, 125
Coffee frosting, 125
Corn, 92
Corn bread, 104
Corn muffins, 104
Corned beef hash, 98
Cottage cheese and onion stuffing, 159
Cranberry sauce, 176, 221
Cream cheese and banana sandwiches on raisin bread, 170
Cream cheese and olive sandwiches, 226
Cream cheese frosting, 130
Cream of chicken soup, 141
Crumbly topping, 120
Cucumber rounds with sour cream dollops, 115
Cucumber rounds with sour cream and caviar, 126
Curried rice, 117

D

Date, celery and cheddar cheese salad, 225
Deviled ham sandwiches, 124
Drop biscuits, 87

E

Easy eggplant bake, 121
Easy lemon crisp cookies, 82
Easy Spinach egg bake, 122
Easy wine spritzers, 95
Egg salad sandwich, 95, 133
Endive and romaine salad with Beth's dressing, 128
English muffin pizzas, 106
Euro- breakfast, 236

F

Fast gravy, 180
Fast turkey pie, 190
Fettucine Alfredo, 189
Franks and beans, 74
Fried eggs, 128
Fresh strawberries, 81
Fruit punch, 226
Fruit salad, 213

G

Garbanzo bean and sweet red bell pepper salad, 180
Gelatin dessert, 206
  with fruit, 187
Graham cracker crust, 116
Grape, orange and pear salad, 143
Grapefruit, 124
Green bean bake, 195
Green beans, 63, 112
Green bell peppers and zucchini, 118
Green peas, 191
Green pepper rings, 75
Green salad #1, 69
Green salad #2, 79
  with blue cheese, 95
  with orange juice dressing, 216
  with shrimp, 122
Green salad #3, 92
Grilled cheese and tomato sandwich, 61
Grilled or pan fried whitefish, 174
Grilled steaks, 91

H

Ham and asparagus roll-ups with Hollandaise sauce, 176, 209
Ham and tomato sandwiches, 109
Ham sandwiches, 119
Ham steaks, 68
Hamburger and rice stir-up, 211
Hash brown potatoes, 225
Hearty baked beans, 229
Hollandaise sauce, 76
Home fried potatoes, 85
Hot dogs and sauerkraut, 102
Hot potato salad, 149
Hungarian golden chicken, 127

I

Ice cream, 64
Iced tea, 64
Ida's apple dessert, 119
Italian lemon ice, 92
Italian sausage, peppers and onions, 192

L

Larisa's strawberries with brown sugar and sour cream
leftover turkey, 224
Lemon dressing, 80

M

Macaroni and cheese with sliced hot dogs, 120
Mashed potatoes, 186
Mashed potatoes and carrots, 238
Meat loaf recipe #1, 63
Meat loaf #2, 123
Melon slices and strawberries, 175
Mini-mixed grill, 182
Mock Hollandaise sauce, 177
Molasses glaze, 68
Mustard sauce, 171

N

Never bake cheese cake, 96

O

Oatmeal, 187
Onion and beet salad, 186
Onion dip, 90
Onion gratinee, 183
Orange juice dressing, 179
Orange slices, 128
Oregano potatoes, 149
Oven boiled steaks, 91
Oven pot roast and vegetables, 127

P

Pancakes, 88
Pan fried hamburgers, 85
Pan fried potatoes, 192
Pan fried steaks, 91
Parsley potatoes, 95
Parsley scrambled eggs, 170
Pasta with cottage cheese and spinach, 122
Peach halves with liqueur, 180
Peanut butter and bacon sandwich, 172
Peanut butter and banana sandwich, 92
Peas and carrots, 150
Poached eggs, 114
Poached whitefish, 110
Poaching liquid, 110
Popcorn, 151
Pork chop and rice casserole, 83
Pork chops, 171
Potato salad, 159
Potatoes and peppers, 108
Pound cake with chocolate sauce and ice cream, 217
Prepared or "store-bought" gelatin, 160

Q

Quick pasta sauce, 79
Quicker broccoli, 88

R

Raisin bread French toast, 172
Rapid corned beef hash, 114
Red flannel eggs,, 212
Red sauce #1, 76
Red sauce #2, 120
Rice, 146, 172
Ricotta cream, 144

Roast beef with oven roasted onions, potatoes and carrots, 178
Roast chicken, 116
Roast pork with oven roasted potatoes, 156
Roast pork and red pepper sandwiches, 132
Roast turkey, 220
Rosemary potatoes, 219
Rum coffee, 144

S

Salmon patties with peas, white sauce, and sliced potatoes, 281
Salmon rice salad, 93
Sandy tarts, 95
Sauce for roasted chicken, 100
Sauce for Swedish meatballs, 193
Sauce for Zippy chicken, 167
Sauce made from cream of asparagus soup, 210
Sauteed apples and bananas, 92
Sauteed mushrooms, 181
Sauteed scallops, 146
Savory baked onions, 175
Scrambled eggs, 73, 108
"Scratch" brownies, 67
"Scratch" corn bread, 105
"Scratch" cranberry sauce, 177
Shepherd's pie, 184
Simple oil and vinegar dressing, 143
Sliced potatoes, 223
Sliced tomatoes with vinaigrette dressing, 75
Sole or whitefish, 224
Spaghetti carbonara, 78
Spinach with curry, 171
Spinach, bacon and mushroom salad, 188
Steaks, 76
Strawberries, 188
Stuffed cherry tomatoes, 158
Stuffed celery sticks with cream and cheddar cheese stuffing, 109
Stuffing for turkey, 220
Surprising "fresh" canned mushroom soup, 152
Swedish meatballs, 193
Swiss cheese and lettuce sandwiches, 176

T

Three cheese macaroni, 119
Three pepper and mozzarella salad, 229
Tira Mi Su #1, 81
Tira Mi Su #2, 143
Toast points, 181
Tomatoes Provencal, 182
Tossed green salad, 184
Tuna, rice, and pepper salad, (Tuna salad #2), 153
Tuna noodle casserole, 85
Tuna salad #1, 66
Turkey hash with poached eggs, 222

U

Uptown pancakes, 88

V

Veal chops "smothered" with onions, 223
Vegetarian stuffed peppers with rice, 217
Vinaigrette dressing, 75

W

Waffles, 81
Waffles with blueberry topping, 155
White bean salad #1, 145
White sauce, 210
Western corn, 77
White sauce, 177

Z

Zippy chicken, 194

Index

A

accessories, 17
  table, 17
alcohol, 10
ale, ales, 207
Alfredo, fettucine, 189
Alice's potato salad, 205, 211
allspice, 51
alternatives
  low fat, 10
  low salt, 10
aluminum roasting pan, 197
always theres™, 142, 197
animal rights, 10
appeal of food, 16
  adding to the, 16
apple, apples, 30, 35, 42, 65, 132, 133, 167, 199, 213, 221, 237
  and bananas, sauteed, 92
  as snack,
  juice, 37
  Baked, 47
  Cortland, 35
  Ida Red, 35,
  Jonathan, 35
  Mackintosh, 35
  Northern Spy, 35
  salad, broccoli and, 239
  sauce, 36
  Winesap, 35
**Apple dessert
  Ida's,**
appliances, 19, 20
  basic, 19
  electrical,, 23
  small, 23
apricots, 133, 207
artichoke hearts, 36, 203, 205
asparagus, 162, 169, 199, 203, 210
Au gratin potatoes, 68
automatic dishwasher, 234, 236
avocados, 162, 169, 212
  with fruit salad, 212

B

Baby carrots, 15
bacon, 32, 34, 38, 52, 70, 132
  and peanut butter sandwiches, 172
  generally, 52
  lettuce and tomato sandwich, 148
  Pan fried, 52
  Microwave, 53
bag, bags, 236
  doggie, 7
  plastic, 236
  trash, 236
bagels, 164, 166, 203
  frozen, 164, 166
bake, 23
baked beans, 156
baked goods, 42
baking
  dishes, 21
    ceramic, 21
    glass, 21
  mix, 12, 30, 36, 41, 112, 164
  powder, 100
  soda, 30
**Baked apples, 47
baked beans, 188, 229
  hearty, 229**
  baked foods,
    Apples, 47
    peaches, 223
    pears, 137, 140, 223
    potatoes, 62, 225
  baking, 17
    dish, ceramic or glass, 17
    items, 17
    mix, 13, 32
    pan, metal, 22
    sheet, 22
balsalmic vinegar, 128, 223
bananas, 15, 35, 123, 132, 133, 167, 170, 199
  peeling, 15
  preparation of, 14
  Sliced
Barbecue, 20
  grill, 20
  need for, 20
  sauce 224
hamburgers, 224
basic, basics
  coffee, 59
  equipment, 9
  skills, 10
  tools, 17
basil, 52, 97, 239
basket, 25
  bread, 25
bay leaf, 127
  straw, 25
beans, 38, 41
  baked, 38
  Boston baked
  canned, 30
  cannelini, 38
  dried, 30, 41
  Great Northern, 38
  green, 18, 38, 174, 201
    canned, 16
    frozen, 38
    stove top, 46
    microwave
  kidney, 38, 41
  Navy, 38, 41
  pinto, 41
  pork and, 38
  vegetarian baked, 38
  white, 38
Bechamel sauce, 210
beef, 32, 98
  chuck, 98
  corned, 198
    sliced, 198
  fresh, 32
  ground, 198
  stew, from scratch, 184
  stock, 39
beer, beers, 166, 204, 213, 225
  coffee cake, 113
beer glasses, 21
beet, beets, 99, 168, 186
  and onion salad, 186
bell peppers, 37, 132, 168, 199, 229, 237
  green, 37, 229, 237

red, 168, 199, 229
and celery sticks, 121
and garbanzo bean salad, 180
yellow, 199, 229
Rings, as snack, 57
beverages, 204, 213
  coffee, hot
  coffee, iced
  milk
  tea, hot
  tea, iced
bibb lettuce, 216
biscuit mix, 30, 41
biscuits
  Drop biscuits ,35
  Drop biscuits, alternative, 35
black bean, corn, and tomato salad, 207, 216
black pepper, 41
  ground, 41
blanch, 23
"blondie, blondies," 66
  mix, 66
blue cheese stuffing, 159
blueberry, blueberries, 167, 169, 206, 216
  pancakes, 206, 216, 217
board, 22
  cutting, 22
"boredom factor," 12
boil, 25
boiled rice, 93
boiler, 20
  double, 20
bologna, 139, 132, 154
bow tie pasta, with scallions, salmon, and tomato, 180
bullion
  chicken, instant, 36, 220
  cube, chicken, 36, 220
bowls, 21
  cereal, 24
  dessert, 24
  mixing, 22
  salad, 24
  soup, 24
  bow tie pasta
Brad's beer bread. 69
braise, 23
bread, 15, 32, 59, 100, 136, 203, 206
  and butter dishes, 21, 64
  basket, 25
  Brad's beer bread, 69
  bread box storage of, 14
  bread boxes, 14
  crumbs, 174, 218, 227
  French, 135, 238
  Italian, 238
  refrigerator storage of, 14
  sliced, preparation of, 14
  sticks, 103, 202, 205
  straw. 25
breakfast, 16
  bake, 148
  potatoes, 72
broccoli, 38, 87, 207
  and apple salad, 239
  fresh, 38
  frozen, 18, 38, 164
  Quicker broccoli,
  broil, 27
broom, 236
broth, 220
  chicken, 220
brown gravy, 14, 179
  for meat loaf, 14, 179
  for roast beef, 179
brown sugar, 38, 120, 128, 223
Brownies, 67, 203, 207 235
  store bought, 69, 235
  from mix, 69, 235
  mix, 69
  "scratch," 67
Brussels sprouts, 155
bucket, 236
buffet, 197, 202
The Big Game
buns, 42
  hamburger, 42
butter, 11, 15, 30, 32, 33, 39, 50, 59, 111, 122, 172, 198, 205, 209
  dish, 25
  sauce, 137
  spreader, 25

C

cabbage, 15, 132
  storage life of, 14
cacciatore, chicken, 237
cake, 100, 129
  carrot, 100, 129
  devil's food, 100
  holder, 20
  Coffee cake, 113
    Beer coffee cake, 113
    mix, 16, 230
  sheet, 207, 230
can opener, 22
Canadian whiskey, 214
candles, 17, 26
candlesticks, 26
canister, 236
  flour, 236
canned foods, 38, 197
  can opener, 22
cantaloupe, 57, 98, 200
capers, 52, 176
caraway seeds, 56
Carbonara, spaghetti, 59
cardamom, 54
carrots, 12, 15, 22, 35, 36, 132
  baby, 15
  cake, 100, 129
  washed and peeled, 14
  Sticks, as snack 22, 61, 178
casseroles, 21
  Pork chop and rice, 33
  Tuna noodle 34
cast iron, 21
  frying pan, 21
catsup, (ketchup) 30, 36
cauliflower, 205, 211
  and carrots, 205, 211
caviar, 100
Ceil's Passover cookies, 168
celery, 35, 36, 42, 52, 64, 100, 109, 132, 133, 163, 216, 218, 220, 227

diced, 210
sticks and bell pepper rings, 121
stuffed, 109
centerpiece, 33
ceramic, 21
  baking dishes, 21
cereal, cereals, 30, 32, 36, 135, 223
  breakfast, 135
  cold, 30, 36
  hot, 30, 36, 103
chairs, 17
cheese, 30, 32, 33, 42, 51, 61, 131, 161, 198, 238
  American, 61
  Asiago, 238
  blue, 238
  cheddar, 30, 33, 140, 131, 161, 198
  or Swiss on crackers, 169
  cottage, 57, 98, 131, 161
  cream, 30, 33. 98, 170, 198, 205
    and banana sandwiches, 167
    and cheddar blend, 64
    and olive sandwiches, 225, 226
  grated, 42
  hot pepper, 198
  locatelli, 42
  mozzarella, 30, 33, 98, 198
  Parmesan, 30, 42, 68, 98
  provolone, 238
  ricotta, 161
  Romano, 42
  process, 33
  Sandwich, grilled, 22
  shredded, 33
  spread, 207, 226
  Swiss, 30, 61, 162, 198, 205
  Sandwiches
    Grilled and tomato, 44
    Wedge of, as snack
cheesecake, 112
  never bake, 112
cheeses, 22
cherry, cherries, 133, 214
  for cocktails, 214
  tomatoes, 108
chestnuts, 221
chicken, 30, 34, 98, 162, 198
  artichoke bake, 94
  bullion, 89
  breast, 198, 215
    boned, 198
  broth, 220
  cacciatore, 237
  canned, 204
  cut up, 34
  canned, 30
  fryer, frying, 34, 132
  livers, 162, 182, 183
  pasta bake, 205, 215
  roast, 116
  zippy, 170
chili bowls, 21
  pepper, 52
chili, 25, 38
chips, 13, 207, 214
  potato, 13, 207
  tortilla, 210, 211
chives, 52
chocolate, 204
  sauce, 204
cholesterol, 70

in eggs, 70
chop, chops, 23, 162
  pork, 162
cinnamon, 30, 42, 53, 97, 113
  toast strips, 205, 208
cloth, 22
  dish, 22
  napkins, 22
  table, 22
cloves, 52, 97
club soda, 214
cocoa, 30, 81
  powder, 30, 81
cocktail party, 197, 213
coffee, 30, 125, 167, 175, 207, 215, 216, 229
  cookies, 125
  frosting, 125
  generally, 21
  ground, 30
  instant, 30
coffee cream, 229
  as Breakfast beverage, 22
  as Snack beverage, 61
coffee cake, 48, 201, 203
  Beer coffee cake, 48 113
coffee liqueur, 81
cola beverage or drink, 205
colander, 22, 82
commercial foods, 12
condiments, 207
convection ovens, 12
conventions, 15
  in table setting, 15
cookie sheet, 21
cookie, cookies,
  Ceil's Passover cookies, 177
  coffee cookies, 58
  dough, 203
  Easy coffee frosting, 58
  Easy lemon crisp, 32
  Sandy tarts, 38
  sheet, 21
  cooking, 20
  methods, 12
  oil, 30, 41
  process, 8
  cool, 23
  corkscrew, 22
  corn, 38, 41, 92
    bread, 104
    "scratch," 105
    flakes, 41
    frozen, 38
    starch, 31
    muffins, 104
    Western, 92
  corned beef hash, 100, 114
    rapid, 114
  counter top, 19
  cover, 21
    saucepan, 21
  crackers, 30, 36, 135, 206
  cranberry, cranberries, 200
    juice, 37, 175
    sauce, 200, 219, 221
      canned, 175, 200
      jellied, 175
      "scratch," 177
    cream, 33, 42, 205
    cheese, this index

soups, 39, 135, 215
  asparagus, 210
  chicken, 141, 215
  mushroom, 39
  sour, 33, 42
crust, 203
pie, 203
cucumber, cucumbers, 98, 132
  rounds, with sour cream dollops, 115
  Sliced, as side dish
cup, cups, 17, 24, 234
  disposable, 234
  in table setting, 17
  measuring, 21
  plastic, 17
cumin, 52
curry, curried, 117, 171
  powder, 100
  spinach with, 171
  rice, 117
cutting board, 25
  plastic, 25

D

dairy products, 11, 32, 197
dates, 200
  dried, 200
  salad, with cheddar cheese, celery, 225
demi tasse set, 23
detergents, 23
  dishwasher, 23
  liquid dish washing, 20
dessert bowls, 21
deviled ham, 100
dice, 24
Dijon mustard, 80
dill weed, 52, 97, 100
dinner, 24
  forks, 24
  knives, 24
  plates, 24
dinners, frozen, 7
dip, dips, 16, 197, 207
  onion, 198
  party, 16,
dish, 20,
  butter, 25
  cloths, 25
  rack, 23, 238
  rags, 23, 238
  towels, 23, 25
  vegetable, 20
  towels, 20
dishes, 14, 233, 234
  disposable, 234
  main, 14
  serving, 14, 20, 23, 24
dishwasher, automatic, 23. 234
  detergent, 23, 237
  liquid, 23, 237
  powdered, 23, 237
  mobile, 20
  under-the-counter, 23
disposable, disposables, 234
  cups, 234
  dishes, 234
  flatware, 234
disposer, 234

in-sink, 234
distilled white vinegar, 41
double boiler, 23
"doggie bag," drainboard, 23
  portable, 23
draining rack, 238
Drambuie, 180
dressing, 20
  French, 40
  Russian, 20
  salad, 20
  vinaigrette, 20
dried soup mixes, 12
  as party mix, 12
  as sauce basic, 12
  as soup, 12
drop biscuits, 87
dustpan, 236

E

Easy eggplant bake, 121
Easy lemon crisp cookies, 82
Easy spinach bake, 138
Easy wine spritzers, 95
eating ideas, healthy 10
egg, eggs, 26, 30, 37, 70, 131, 162, 218
  beaten, 227
  generally, 26
  fried, 70, 131
  hard boiled, 70, 218
  Poached, 70, 206
  Red flannel, 205
  Scrambled, 28
  Salad, 36
  Salad sandwich, 36, 89
  yolks, 209
slicer, 23
egg beater, 22
eggplant, 98, 121
  Eggplant bake, 121
elbow macaroni or pasta, 135
electric
  appliances, small 23
  food processor, 22
  mixer, 22
endive, 98, 129
English muffins, 100, 136, 166, 175, 203, 206
equipment, 9, 20
  basic, 9, 20
evaporated milk, 165
expiration dates, 32, 38

F

fast
  gravy, 180
  turkey pie, 190
fat, 11
  low, 11
  high, 11
  lower, 11
fats, 11
fennel seed, 211
fish, 11, 15, 23, 30, 32, 34, 198
  canned, 30
  filet, 34
  flounder, 172

fresh, 32, 34
  poached, 109
  rinsing of, 14
  salmon, 30, 34, 199
  storage of, 14
  tuna, 30
  Salad I, 66
  Salad sandwich adaptation, 66
  Noodle casserole, 85
  whitefish, 110
  Poached, 110
fixture, fixtures, 19
  basic, 19
flatware, 16, 24, 234
  disposable, 234
flounder, 172
flour, 23, 38, 210, 239
  sifter, 23
flowers, 17, 32
food, foods, 12, 16, 38
  appeal, 16
  convenience, 12
  frozen, 12
  processors 12, 22
    electric, 22
  preparation process, 234
fork, 17, 21, 24, 25
  in table setting, 17
  for cooking, 18
  serving, 25
forks, 17, 24, 25
  dinner, 25
  salad, 25
frankfurters, franks, 74
  And beans, 74
freezer, 19
  compartment, 19
French, 41
  dressing, 41
fresh foods, 32, 36
frozen, 12
  broccoli, 18
  dinners 7
  food, 12
  juice, 134
  vegetables, 15
frosting, 125, 130
  coffee, 125
  cream cheese, 130
fruit, fruits, 30, 198, 206, 211
  apples, this index
  bananas, this index
  canned, 30
  cantaloupe, this index
  cup, 206
  dried, 31
  frozen, 30
  juices, 134
  grapes, this index
  grapefruit, this index
  juice, juices, 30, 37, 164 200
  oranges, 37
  peaches, this index
  pears, this index
  punch, 200, 209
  salad, 213
  strawberries, 37
fry, 23
frying pan, 18
  cast iron, 18

nonstick, 18
furniture, 20
  basic, 20

G

garbage, 236
garbanzo beans, 168
  and bell pepper salad, 180
garlic, 15, 30, 36, 52, 80
  chopped, 224
  clove of, 36
  fresh, 30, 37
  head of, 36
  minced, 174
  pantry storage of, 14
  powdered, 30, 37
garnish, garnishes
  basics, 84
  generally, 108
gelatin, 206
  dessert, 187, 206
gin, 213
ginger ale, 214
ginger, ground, 52
gizzards, 219
  turkey, 219
glass, glasses, 17, 24, 213
  baking dishes, 21
  for cocktail party, 214
  in table setting, 17
  beer, 24
  juice, 24
  "old fashioned," 24
  on-the-rocks, 24
glazes
  Molasses, 50
goods, 42
  baked, 42
gourmet, 10
granola mix, 169
grape, grapes, 142, 169, 238
  fresh, 168, 172, 188
  jam, 39
  jelly, 165
  juice, 37
  seedless, 238
  white, 213
grapefruit, 37, 98, 124, 206
  juice, 37
  orange and pear salad, 143
  fresh squeezed, 37
  frozen concentrated, 37
grater, 22
grated, 22
  carrots, 22
  cheeses, 22
gratinee, 183
  onion, 183
gravy, 14
  brown, 14
  fast, 180
  for meat loaf, 14
  for roast beef, 179
  turkey, 224
green beans, 18, 38, 46, 63, 112, 132, 164, 219
green bell pepper, 37
  and zucchini, 118
Rings, as snack, 75

green olives, 73
green peas, 191
green salads, 205, 216
Green salad #1, 50, 205
  with shrimp, 122
  #2, with blue cheese, 95
grill, 20, 24
  barbecue, 20
  method of cooking, 20
Grilled cheese and tomato sandwich, 61
Grilled tomato, corned beef, and mozzarella sandwich, 206
Grilled whitefish, 168
ground beef, 224
ground cloves, 36

H

ham, 30, 37, 38, 132, 140, 197, 198, 206, 208, 209, 227, 228
  and tomato sandwiches, 109
  Asparagus and ham roll ups, baked, 207, 228
  canned, 30, 228
  country, 228
  deviled, 100, 124
    sandwiches, 124
  fresh, 228
  sandwiches, 137, 140
  sliced, 199
  smoked, 228
  Steaks, 68
    Stove top, 69
    Oven baked, 69
hamburger, hamburgers 34, 211
  and rice stir-up, 205
  basics, 84
  buns, 42, 203
  pan fried, 85, 237
  rolls, 203
hand soap, 23
hash brown potatoes, 225
hash, turkey, 206
healthy eating ideas, 10
herbs, 29, 38
high fat, 10
high salt, 10
holidays, 33
Hollandaise sauce, 208, 209
home fried potatoes, 85
honey, 65
hors d'ouevres, 226
horseradish, 52
hot cereal, 103, 223
hot dogs (frankfurters), 34, 118, 120
  and sauerkraut, 118
hot pads, 19
hot pepper, 100, 221, 224
hot pepper cheese, tomato and lettuce sandwiches, 216
hotcakes (see pancakes)
hot potato salad, 157
Hungarian golden chicken, 149

I

ice, 19
  Italian, lemon, 107

ice cream, 169
  store bought, 64, 216
ice cube, 19
  trays, 193
Iced tea, 64
Ida's apple dessert, 119
ideas for leftovers, 9
ingredients, 8, 13, 41, 55
inventory, 35
Italian sausage, 162, 169, 192
  with peppers and onions, 192

J

jam, 30, 37, 39
  strawberry, 30, 39
jelly, 30, 39
juice, juices, 135, 164, 201, 206, 211, 214, 225
  fruit, 164, 201
  frozen, 164, 201
  tomato, 83
  vegetable, 138
  glasses, 21
  lemon, 209

K

ketchup (catsup), 38
kitchen, 17, 29, 197, 233, 234
  cleanup, 233
  terms, 23
  towels, 17
knife, knives, 17, 18, 21, 24
  bread, 19
  carving, 19
  chopping, 19
  dinner, 24
  work, 22
  in table setting, 15
  paring, 19, slicing, 19

L

labels, 41
ladyfingers, 81
leftovers, 9, 21
  ideas for, 9
leftovers, 9, 11, 13
  legs, 220
  turkey, 220
lemon, lemons, 35, 42, 163, 209, 211, 216
  dressing, 80
  ice, Italian, 107
  juice, 209, 211, 216
  sliced, as garnish, 172
lettuce, 35, 69, 175, 200
  Boston, 98
  iceberg, 69
  Romaine, 69
lighting, 16
  subdued, 16
liqueur, 180
  and peach halves, 180
liquid, 20, 203
  detergent, 20, 203
  dishwasher, 20, 233

Never Cooked Before/Gotta Cook Now™ 247

list, shopping 29
list, stocking up 29
livers, chicken, 182
low fat, 11, 39
  cream of mushroom soup, 39
  low fat alternatives, 11
lower fat, 11
low salt, 11, 39
  cream of mushroom soup, 39
lower salt, 10
lox, 175
luncheon meat, 30, 98
  canned, 30, 98

M

macaroni (see pasta, this index)
  three cheese, 119
  and cheese, (leftover), with sliced hot dogs, 120
main dishes, 13
maple syrup, 65, 225
margarine, 33, 132, 198
marinated artichoke hearts, 99
marmalade, 39
  orange, 39
mashed potatoes, 186
  and carrots, 239
matzoh cake meal, 165, 177
mayonnaise, 31, 37, 41
meal, matzoh cake, 165, 177
measuring, 21
  cups, 21
  spoons, 21
meat, 198
  balls, Swedish, 193
  red 11
meat loaf, 14
  Meat loaf #1, 63
  #2, 103, 123
melon, 205, 208
  and strawberries, 205, 208
menus, 9, 29, 55
methods, cooking 12
microwave, 7, 12, 17, 52
  oven, 17. 23, 52
  second-hand, 23
  popcorn, 7
milk, 31, 32, 59, 197
  condensed, 37
  evaporated, 37, 165
  percent butterfat in, 32
  fresh, 31
  powdered, 31
  skim, 32
mince, 24
mini-salmon cakes, 225
mix
  baking, 12, 13
  onion soup, 12
mixed salad greens, 12
mixer, electric, 22
mixer, mixers,
  for drinks, 214
mixing
  bowls, 22
  tools, 22
molasses, 41
  Glaze, 68
mop, 236

for kitchen floor, 236
  sponge, 236
mozzarella, 207
  cheese, 207
  salad, 207
muffin, muffins, 203
  English, 136, 166, 203
  tins, 233
mugs, 21
mushroom, mushrooms, 37, 133, 163, 169, 184, 237
  fresh, 39
  sauteed, 181
  soup, cream of, 39
mustard, 40, 52
  brown, 40
  Chinese, 40
  Dijon, 40, 80
  dry, 31, 40
  prepared, 31, 40, 80
  sauce, 167, 171
  yellow, 40

N

napkin, napkins, 17, 25, 32
  cloth, 25
  paper, 25
nectarine, 133, 195, 200, 216
noodles, 169
nutmeg, 52, 97, 100, 171
nuts, 200, 214
  mixed, 214

O

oatmeal, 165, 169
oils, 11, 38, 41, 172, 215
  corn, 41
  olive, 41, 80, 219, 225, 237
  soy, 41
olive, olives, 204, 214, 216
  and cream cheese sandwiches, 225
omelet, 70
onion, onions, 15, 31, 35, 36, 133, 163, 201, 211, 215, 216, 218, 220, 223, 226, 227, 237
  and beet salad, 168
  and strawberry salad, 169
  dip, 90
  flakes, 31
  Green, 35, 36, 133
  fresh, 37
  gratinee, 168, 183
  oven roasted, 178
  pantry storage of, 14
  purple, 35, 133
  red (purple) 211, 237
  scallions, 201
  soup mix, 12
  dried, 12
  savory baked onions, 172
  sliced onions, 176
  yellow, 35
  Vidalia, 35
on-the-rocks glasses, 21
optional ingredients, 11
orange, oranges, 36, 178, 207, 213, 221, 236
  juice, 37, 59

dressing, 216
  fresh squeezed, 37
  frozen concentrated, 37
  peel, 69
 Sliced
  with liqueur,
  oregano, 52, 80, 169, 175, 239
 oven, ovens, 12, 20
  convection, 12
  microwave, 12, 20
  toaster, 20
 oysters, 221

P

packages, 14
  smallest sizes, 14
pancake, pancakes, 88, 202
  basic, with baking mix
  Uptown
 pancake turner, 22
 pan, pans, 21, 22, 233, 237
  baking, 22
  ceramic, 22
  frying, 21, 236
  fried potatoes, 169, 202
  fried whitefish, 169
  cast iron, 21
  roasting, 233, 236
  aluminum, 197
pantry, 197
paper, 25, 227
  napkins, 25, 31, 37
  plates, 215, 227
  towels, 25, 31, 37
paprika, 52, 136
Parmesan cheese, 167, 183
parsley, 36, 44, 52, 134, 215,
  220, 221, 239
  chopped fresh, as garnish, 73
  scrambled eggs, 167
  potatoes, 109, 111
Passover cookies, 177
pasta, 31, 37, 135, 202
  American spaghetti
  bake, with chicken, 215
  Bow tie, with salmon and
  scallion sauce, 134, 180
  Quick sauce for, 79
  sauce basics, 75
pastry tube, 23
patties, salmon, 219
peach, peaches, 40, 133, 199, 207
  baked, 207
  canned, 40
  fresh, 40
  sliced, 206, 216
  halves with Schnapps, 180
peanut 39, 105, 168
  butter, 39, 168, 172, 204, 206, 219
  and banana sandwich, 82
pears, 133, 199
  As snack
peas, 37, 38, 164, 218, 224
  and carrots, 150
  canned, 37
  fresh, 37
  frozen, 37
peelers, 20

potato or vegetable, 20
pepper, 22, 37
  black, 31, 239, 240
  corns, 52
  ground red, 97
  hot red, 31
  hot red pepper sauce, 212
  shaker, 25
peppers, 31, 36, 163, 199
  bell, 31, 36, 37, 199
  green, 31, 36, 163, 199
  other colors, 31, 199
  red, 31, 163, 199
  Green bell pepper rings
pickles, 73, 204
pie, 203
  crust, 203
  fast turkey, 190
  pumpkin, 204
pimento, chopped, 74
pinch, 30
pitcher, 22
planning ahead, 9
plastic, 17, 22
  cups, 17, 227
  cutting board, 22
  drink stirrers, 215, 227
  flatware, 227
  glasses, 215, 227
  plates, 17
  scouring pad, 20
  trash bags, 236
plate. plates, 13, 17
  dinner, 17, 24
  in table setting, 17
  salad, 24
platter, 14
  serving, 14, 24
plum, plums, 199, 213, 216
poach, 24
  poached eggs, 222
  poached whitefish, 110
  poaching liquid, 110
popcorn, 7, 134, 161, 167
  popcorn, microwave, 7
pork, 32, 38, 98, 167, 171
  and beans, 38
  bacon, this index
  chops, 34, 167, 171
    and rice casserole, 83
    with mustard sauce, 167, 171
  fresh, 32
  ham, this index
  roast, 133
  Pork chop and rice casserole,
potato, potatoes, 15, 36, 133, 163, 201, 211, 212
  Alice's potato salad, 211
  and carrots, mashed, 239
  Au gratin, 49
  Baked, 219, 221
    conventional oven, 219
    microwave, 219
  Boiled
  Breakfast, pan fried
    chip, chips, 13, 202
    Home fried, with onions
    oven roasted, 178
    pantry storage of, 14
  Parsleyed
    redskin, 163, 211

Never Cooked Before/Gotta Cook Now™ 249

Rosemary, 163, 219
  russet, 133, 163
  Salad, 207, 229
  Sliced, 207
  Yukon gold, 133
potato peeler, 22
pot holders, 13, 22
pots, 20
pound cake, 99, 144, 216
poultry, 11, 15, 23, 32, 34
  fresh, 32
  rinsing of, 14
  storage of, 14
powdered
  dishwasher detergent, 237
  sugar, 135, 172
preparation, 9
prepared foods, 38
preserves, 39
  strawberry, 39
presentation, 9, 15
  in table setting, 15
pressure cooker, 23
pretzel pretzels, 134, 165, 169, 172, 214
  sticks, 134
processors, food, 12
produce, 32
pudding, 202, 206
  mix, 202
  chocolate
  vanilla, 202
pumpkin, 204, 219
  pie, 204, 219, 221
  filling, 204
punch, 226
  fruit, 226

Q

Quick pasta sauce, 79
Quicker broccoli, 88

R

rack, 20
  dish, 20
radishes, 201,
rag, 20
  dish, 20
raisin, raisins, 31, 37, 100, 167, 172, 221
  raisin bread, 166
    French toast, 167, 172
recipes, 9, 10, 11, 55
  difficult, 16
  easiest, 16
  vegetarian, 11
red bell pepper and garbanzo bean salad, 180
red meat, 11
refrigerator, 13, 15, 20, 234, 235, 237
  coldest part of, 20
  necessity for, 19
relishes, 207, 227
replacement, 16
  of one food for another, 16
ribs, 38
rice, 11, 14, 38, 42, 83, 134, 166, 172, 202, 205, 207, 211
  and hamburger stir-up, 205
  and pork chop casserole,

as "soup stretcher," 11
  brown, 42
  instant, 42
  white, 42
ricotta cream, 144
roast, 24, 206, 219
  beef and gravy, 168
  beef with roasted onions, potatoes, and carrots, 178
  pork, 132, 139, 154
  and red bell pepper sandwiches, 156
  turkey, 197, 206, 219
roasting pan, 233
  aluminum, 197
rolls, 168, 203, 205, 206, 225
  hamburger, 203
Romaine lettuce, 216
Rosemary, 52, 211, 219, 223
rum, 81, 214
  coffee, 144
Russian dressing
rye whiskey, 214

S

saffron, 52
sage, 52, 97, 171, 221, 223
salad, 12
  basics, 79
  broccoli and apple, 239
  composee, salade, 80
  dressing, 40
    French, 40
  forks, 21
  greens, 12
    mixed, 12
  plates, 21
salads
  Egg salad
  Sandwich
  garbanzo bean and red bell pepper, 180
  generally,
  Green salad #1, 50
  Tomato, with vinaigrette
    dressing
  Tossed green, 184
  Tuna fish, 48
salmon, 39, 218
  canned, 218
  with Bowtie pasta and scallions, 180
  mini-salmon cakes, 227
  patties, with peas and sliced potatoes, 218
  and rice salad, 93
salsa, 204
salt, 10, 11, 25, 31, 42, 83, 239, 240
  iodized, 37, 42
  low, 11, 39
  lower, 10
  shaker, 25
sandwiches
  Cream cheese and olive, 207
  deviled ham, 124
  Egg salad
  Grilled cheese and tomato, 44
  meat loaf # 1,
  Peanut butter and bacon
  Tuna fish salad, 48
  turkey salad, 207
sauce,

Never Cooked Before/Gotta Cook Now™ 250

apple, 224
barbecue, 224
base, 12
chocolate, 204, 216
cranberry, 204
for Swedish meatballs, 153
from condensed soup mix, 209, 210
from dried soup mix, 12
Hollandaise, 202
Mock Hollandaise, 210
Pasta,
Quick pasta,
Red sauce # 1
Tomato, 204
for meat loaf, 14
White,
spaghetti, 40
saucer, 24
saucepan, saucepans 21,
cover, 21
sauerkraut, 118
sausage, 162, 168, 221
links, 132
pork, 132
turkey, 132
saute, sauteed, 24, 181
sauteed mushrooms, 181
scallops, 148
scald, 24
scallions, 98, 133, 201
Scotch whiskey, 213
"scratch"
beef stew, 185
cranberry sauce, 177
scrambled eggs, 225
service, 13
family style, 13
restaurant style, 13
serving, 13, 21, 22
dishes, 13, 14, 21
fork, 22
shaker, 22
pepper, 22
salt, 22
sheets, 19
baking or cookie, 19
sherbet, 169
Shepherd's pie, 175, 184
sherry, 175
shopping lists, 13, 31
shortening, 31, 69
shred, 24
shrimp, 100, 122
cocktail, 100
in sauce, 100, 122
sifter, 20,
flour, 20
simmer, 27
simple oil and vinegar dressing, 143
sink, 20, 233, 234
kitchen, 20
six steps to a "winning meal," 12
skills, basic 10
slice, sliced, 24
bread, 15
peaches, 213
potatoes, 217
tomatoes with vinaigrette dressing, 75
turkey, 207
slicer, 20

egg, 20
small sizes of food packages, 14
soap, 20
hand, 20
sole, 198
filets, 198
soup, soups, 12, 21, 30, 37
bowls, 21
canned, 31
condensed, 39
cream of mushroom, 39
dried, 31
from dried soup mix, 12
low-fat, 39
low salt, 39
mix, mixes, 12, 42
dry, 42
dried, 12
sorbet, 98, 169
sour cream, 12 42, 97, 198, 205, 210
sparkling water, 206, 213, 219
spatula, 22
flexible, 22
spaghetti, 40
sauce, 40
spatula, 19
flexible, 19
spices, 29, 55, 135
spinach, 133, 144, 164, 201, 207, 223
egg bake, 144
frozen, 133, 202
chopped, 133
mushroom, and bacon salad, 169, 188
spirits, alcoholic, 11
sponge, 23, 237
spoon, spoons, 21. 24, 24
in table setting, 17
large for cooking, 18
mixing, 19
serving, 24, 25
soup, 25
spreader, 25
butter, 25
sprouts, 206, 216
Brussels, 206, 216
squash, 99, 201
frozen, 201
staples, 29, 38, 55, 197
steaks
beef, 91
grilled, 91
Delmonico, 34
filet, 35
New York Strip, 34
T-bone, 34
oven broiled
pan fried, 91
ham, 68
stove top, 68
oven baked, 68
steam, 28
stew, 28
stir fry, 28
storage items, 18
stove, 20
strawberries, 37, 39, 188, 133, 205, 216
fresh, 37
frozen, 37
jam, 39
jelly, 39

Never Cooked Before/Gotta Cook Now™ 251

preserves, 39
  Larisa's, with sugar, 205
stuffed cherry tomatoes, 156
stuffed peppers, 206
  vegetarian, with rice, 206
stuffing, 202
  mix, 166
  for turkey, 202
sugar, 11, 31, 172, 221
  brown, 31, 38, 42, 128
  powdered, 172
  white, 31, 42
Swedish meat balls, 169, 193
  sauce for, 193
Swiss cheese, 168
  and lettuce sandwiches, 168, 176
syrups, 38
system,
  cleanup, 233

T

table, 13, 19
table top, 17
table cloths, 17, 25
table setting, 16, 17
table spoons, 29
tangerine, 201, 207, 221
conventions, 17
Tarts, sandy
tea, 169, 202, 205, 207, 211, 216, 225
  bags, 31
  basics, 59
  generally, 59
  Iced, 47, 205
  instant,
  teaspoons, 21, 28
terms, kitchen, 19
three bean salad, 38
thyme, 52, 127
timing, 9
tins, muffin, 233
tips, 9
tira mi su
  #1, 81
  #2, 143
toast, 28, 173, 180, 206, 207, 216, 225
  points, 180
toaster oven, 23
  second-hand, 23
tomato, tomatoes, 37, 40, 98, 133, 164, 169, 201, 206, 221, 237
  and artichoke salad, 205
  and lettuce sandwiches, 206
  and mozzarella sandwiches, 221
  canned, 40, 239
  crushed, 40
  juice, 83
  whole, 40
  cherry, 133
  in Grilled cheese sandwich, 44
  juice, 40
  paste, 106
  Provencal, 182
  sauce, 14, 41 204, 211
  Sliced, 168, 216
    with vinaigrette
tools, 19
  basic, 19

mixing, 22
topping, 134
  whipped, 134
tortilla, 205
  chips, 205
  and salsa, 205, 213
tossed green salad #2, 79
towels, 20
  dish, 20
  paper, 25
trash, 236
  bags, 236
  plastic, 236
trivet, 25
tumblers, 24
tuna, 39, 47, 135, 204
  albacore, 39
  chunk, 39
  dark, 39
  in oil, 39
  in water, 39
  Noodle casserole, 86
  rice and red pepper salad, 153
  Salad, 48
  solid, 39
  white, 39
turkey, 162 197, 198, 221
  breast, 197, 199, 201
  frozen, 199
  hash, 206
  leftover, 222
  roast, 197
  salad sandwiches, 225
  turner, 22
  pancake 22

U

uptown pancakes, 88
utensils, 15, 17, 20, 23
  specialty, 23
  in table setting, 15
  cooking, 17

V

vanilla, 52, 112, 205
  extract, 52, 112
  pudding, 205
veal, 123, 199
  chops, 204
  smothered, with onions, 207, 223
vegetables
  beans, this index
  green beans, this index
  carrots, this index
  frozen, 15
  juice, 135
  peas, this index
  potatoes, this index
  storage of, 14
  tomatoes, this index
  vegetarian recipes, 11
    stuffed peppers, 206, 216
vermouth, 215
  dry, 214
  sweet, 214
vinegar, 16, 41, 202, 239

balsalmic, 135, 202, 225
　distilled, 41
　flavored, 41, 239
　white, 41, 216
vodka, 213

W

waffles, 38, 169
　frozen, 133, 169
　with blueberry topping, 155
watermelon, 134, 156
water, 12
　as "soup stretcher," 12
　mineral,
　running, 19
whipped, whipping, 134
　cream, 40, 134
　topping, 134
whisk, 22
　wire, 22, 206, 225
white
　beans, 135
　bean salad #1, 145
　bread, 166
　wine, 166
white fish, 198, 223
　filets, 110
　　poached, 110
　fresh, 198
　frozen, 198
white vinegar, 41
　distilled, 41
wine, 11, 168
　spritzers, 95
　glasses, 21
　red, 127, 213
　white, 168, 206, 213
"winning meal," six steps to a, 12
wok, 28
Worcestershire sauce, 204
work space, 19
　flat, 19

X-Y

yams, 15
　pantry storage of, 14
yogurt, 12, 42, 97, 132, 198
Yukon gold potatoes, 133

Z

Zippy chicken, 169
zucchini, 99, 109, 118

Never Cooked Before/Gotta Cook Now™ 253

Order Form

Order Additional Copies of **Never Cooked Before/Gotta Cook Now!**™ for your friends!

Please send ____(quantity) copy(ies) of *Never Cooked Before/Gotta Cook Now!*™ to me at the following address:

Name_____

Street_____Apt._____

City_____State_____

Enclosed is $15.95 plus $3.00 for shipping and handling for each book. Michigan residents add 6% sales tax, or $1.14.

Total amount $_____.___

__Check enclosed in the amount of _____.___

__Please charge my MasterCard___Visa___.

Number_____Exp. date_____

Billing address for charge card (if different than shipping address)

_____

_____

Thank you for your order. Mail to:

Countinghouse Press, Inc., 6632 Telegraph Road, Suite 311, Bloomfield Hills, MI 48301 U. S. A.

or fax to: 248.642.7192.

Order Form

Order Additional Copies of **Never Cooked Before/Gotta Cook Now!**™ for your friends!

Please send ____(quantity) copy(ies) of *Never Cooked Before/Gotta Cook Now!*™ to me at the following address:

Name_____

Street_____Apt._____

City_____State_____

Enclosed is $15.95 plus $3.00 for shipping and handling for each book. Michigan residents add 6% sales tax, or $1.14.

Total amount $_____.___

__Check enclosed in the amount of _____.___

__Please charge my MasterCard___Visa___.

Number_____Exp. date_____

Billing address for charge card (if different than shipping address)

_____

_____

Thank you for your order. Mail to:

Countinghouse Press, Inc., 6632 Telegraph Road, Suite 311, Bloomfield Hills, MI 48301 U. S. A.

or fax to: 248.642.7192.

Notes